THE STORY OF THE BIBLE

THE STORY OF
THE BIBLE

A Popular Account of How it Came to Us

BY

SIR FREDERIC KENYON
G.B.E., K.C.B., F.B.A., F.S.A.

With Eight Plates

LONDON
JOHN MURRAY, ALBEMARLE STREET, W.

First Edition	.	.	January 1936
Reprinted	.	.	February 1936
Reprinted	.	.	May 1936
Reprinted	.	.	December 1942
Reprinted	.	.	July 1944
Reprinted	.	.	February 1947
Reprinted	.	.	September 1949

Made and Printed in Great Britain by
Butler & Tanner Ltd., Frome and London

CONTENTS

CHAP.   PAGE

I THE BIBLE AND RECENT DISCOVERIES . . 1

II THE OLD TESTAMENT 6

III HOW THE BOOKS OF THE NEW TESTAMENT WERE WRITTEN 20

IV FROM MANUSCRIPT TO PRINT . . . 38

V THE ENGLISH BIBLE 47

VI THE SEARCH FOR MANUSCRIPTS . . . 55

VII THE REVISION OF THE TEXT . . . 69

VIII THE AGE OF DISCOVERIES 87

IX THE AGE OF DISCOVERIES (continued): THE CHESTER BEATTY PAPYRI . . . 108

X THE POSITION TO-DAY 127

APPENDIX I. THE PRINCIPAL MANUSCRIPTS AND VERSIONS OF THE GREEK BIBLE . 145

APPENDIX II. THE PEDIGREE OF THE NEW TESTAMENT TEXT 150

INDEX 155

LIST OF ILLUSTRATIONS

FACING
PAGE

CODEX SINAITICUS: END OF ST. LUKE AND BEGIN-
NING OF ST. JOHN.* FOURTH CENTURY   14

PAPYRUS ROLL: LOUVRE HYPERIDES . . . 15

PAPYRUS CODEX: CHESTER BEATTY PAPYRUS IX † 28

A PAGE FROM ERASMUS'S EDITION OF THE NEW
TESTAMENT, 1516* 29

TITLE-PAGE TO PART I FROM COVERDALE'S TRANS-
LATION OF THE BIBLE, 1535 * 48

TITLE-PAGE TO KING JAMES'S, OR THE AUTHORISED
VERSION, 1611 * 49

CHESTER BEATTY PAPYRUS I: GOSPELS AND ACTS.
THIRD CENTURY † 120

CHESTER BEATTY PAPYRUS II: PAULINE EPISTLES.
EARLY THIRD CENTURY † 121

PEDIGREE IN TABULAR FORM OF THE HISTORY OF
THE BIBLE TEXT 150

* *By permission of the Authorities of the British Museum.*
† *„   „   „ Messrs. Emery Walker Ltd.*

THE BIBLE AND RECENT DISCOVERIES

CHAPTER I

THE BIBLE AND RECENT DISCOVERIES

DURING the last few years the Bible and questions
relating to its text have been very much before the
eyes of the public. The purchase of the great
Codex Sinaiticus revived the romantic story of its
discovery, together with various foolish rumours
affecting its genuineness; while the enthusiasm
shown by the general public of all classes and in
all parts of the world proved once again the attach-
ment of the English-speaking peoples to the Bible.
To this has been added the discovery of the Chester
Beatty papyri, a group of manuscripts of many of
the books of both Testaments, imperfect, it is true,
but of substantial size, and older by a century or
more than the oldest manuscripts (other than very
small fragments) hitherto known, and throwing
new light on the conditions in which these books
were originally written and circulated. And then,
still more recently, has come the discovery of some
fragments of a new Gospel, different from the

1

four which we know, but unquestionably of a date in or very shortly after the Apostolic age, which remind us of a time when other records of our Lord's life were in circulation, besides those which were ultimately accepted as authoritative.

In view of all this new material, it may be of interest to make a general survey of it, and to consider what we now know about the way in which the Bible has come down to us. The idea of a Bible accurately handed down without variation from the earliest times has gone. The Bible has a human history as well as a divine inspiration. It is a history full of interest, and it is one which all those who value their Bible should know, at least in outline, if only that they may be able to meet the criticisms of sceptics and the ignorant. We know more about it now than any previous generation has known; and in this short history an attempt will be made to give in intelligible language the results at which scholars have been arriving in the light of the latest discoveries.

The last two generations have been as fruitful of discoveries in archæology (in the widest sense of that term) as the period of the Renaissance was in the field of literature, or the Elizabethan age in geographical exploration. Whole new civilizations have been brought to light—the Sumerian,

2

the Assyrian, the Mycenæan, the Cretan, the Hittite, the Mayan—which have added new chapters to history and art; while our knowledge even of countries so familiar as Greece and Palestine, the cradles of our civilization, has been vastly extended. We can read ancient history in a new light, and with a better comprehension how men lived and thought in those remote days. Ancient traditions have in many cases been justified as against the excessive scepticism of the middle of the nineteenth century; but they have been justified by being made intelligible, and by being put into their proper relation to history. Criticism, instead of being merely negative, has become constructive; and by facing the new facts with an open mind we can, without any subversion of fundamental beliefs, establish our knowledge on a firmer basis, and interpret it in a fresher and more living light.

Of no department of knowledge is this more true than of that which deals with the books of the Bible; and none is more interesting to Englishmen, to whom, since the sixteenth century, the Bible has been the book of books, and whose whole thought, language, and literature are deeply tinged with its words and its teaching. The discoveries of the last hundred years, and increasingly those of the last fifty, have greatly widened

3

and deepened our knowledge of Palestine and of its relations with the neighbouring countries, and have enabled us to read the Hebrew literature, not as an isolated phenomenon, but in relation to the circumstances which gave it birth, and have vastly increased our knowledge of its origins and of the manner in which it was recorded. It is of this latter branch of the subject that the present volume will treat. The Bible being to us what it is, it is of the highest importance that we should be satis-fied of the authenticity of the title-deeds of our faith; that we should be able to accept them, not with a blind and unintelligent belief, but with a clear understanding of the manner in which the several books came into existence, and of the means by which they have been handed down to us. The history of the Bible text is a romance of literature, though it is a romance of which the consequences are of vital import; and thanks to the succession of discoveries which have been made of late years, we know more about it than of the history of any other ancient book in the world.

For the vast majority of English-speaking people, the Bible is the English Authorised Version, first published in 1611. But everybody knows that this is not the original language of the Bible; and as soon as one begins to think about it, various

4

questions present themselves. From what sort of texts was the translation of 1611 made ? How had these texts been handed down ? Were they accurate representations of the works as originally written by the authors of the books of the Old and New Testaments ? What evidence have we about it ? Why was it thought necessary, in the latter part of the nineteenth century, to make a Revised Version? What is the relation of the Revised Version to the Authorised ? And why are the margins of the Revised Version full of references to alternative readings which are said to be found in " ancient authorities " ? What are these ancient authorities, and what is their importance ? How shall we judge which of these alternatives is to be preferred ? These are the questions to which it will be attempted to provide answers in the present book, based upon the most recent discoveries and what seems to be the most reasonable interpretation of them.

CHAPTER II

THE OLD TESTAMENT

LET us take first the Old Testament, before passing on to the New, of which there will be more to say.

It is a matter of common knowledge that, broadly speaking, the books of the Old Testament were originally written in Hebrew, and those of the New Testament in Greek; and the first thing to be remembered is that for by far the greater part of the period which separates us from the dates when the several books of the Bible were first written, every copy of them had to be written by hand. Printing was first invented in Europe in 1454; and the Hebrew Old Testament first appeared in print in 1488, and the Greek New Testament in 1516. Before these dates we are entirely dependent on manuscripts, i.e. handwritten copies; and since it is impossible to copy great quantities of writing without making mistakes, and since also, as we shall see, copyists were not always very particular about exact accuracy, and editors deliberately

6

altered what they thought was either erroneous or obscure, it results that no two manuscripts are ever exactly alike. During these hundreds of years, therefore (nearly 1,400 years in the case of the New Testament, and much more in the case of the Old), we are dependent upon manuscripts, all of which have strayed more or less from the true originals; and from the thousands of manuscripts which have survived we have to determine, as best we can, what was the original form of each passage. As a rule, the older the manuscript the greater the chances of its being correct, though this is a rule to which there are many exceptions; and one of the welcome results of recent discoveries is to give us earlier copies of many of the books than were known before. The Bible is not unique in these respects; the same conditions applied to all books before the invention of printing. The main difference is that we have far more manuscripts, and far older, of the Bible than of other ancient books; on the other hand, as will appear later, the conditions under which the books of the Bible, and especially of the New Testament, were produced and circulated caused special difficulties, which complicate the task of the modern scholar who tries to determine the true original text.

Far less is known of the origins of the Old

Testament books than of those of the New, because of their greater antiquity. A word should be said about their dates.[1] The books of the Prophets, no doubt, go back to the lives of their respective authors, ranging from the eighth century B.C. in the case of Amos, Isaiah, Micah and Hosea, to the fifth century in the case of Malachi; though all seem to have been subject to considerable editorial alterations and additions, and the book which bears the name of Daniel must be later. The poetical books include compositions of very various dates, from the time of David to the second century. The historical books present greater difficulties, and the opinions of scholars vary considerably. The books of the Pentateuch were known from an early period as "the books of Moses"; but they nowhere claim his authorship, and are rather books about him than by him. Scholars agree that these books have been put together out of several earlier narratives, and that they were finally edited about the time of Ezra (early fourth century B.C.). This, of course, does not, in itself, affect their accuracy as records, any more than when a historian to-day writes a history

[1] For a recent summary of contemporary views on these, see Oesterley and Robinson, *An Introduction to the Books of the Old Testament* (London, S.P.C.K., 1934).

of Alfred or Elizabeth on the basis of older records. The documents on which the Pentateuch and the other historical books are based go back to much earlier periods than the dates at which the books were written in their present form; and here recent discoveries have done not a little to help us.

About the middle of the nineteenth century there was a period when it was often maintained that writing was unknown in the time of Moses and the Judges and the earlier kings, and consequently that the narratives of these early periods could not be based on authentic records. This disbelief in the antiquity of writing has been completely disproved by the discoveries of the last century. First of all, in 1852 and 1853 Henry Layard and his assistant Rassam discovered the libraries of the kings of Assyria at Nineveh, which contained hundreds of tablets of baked clay (the form of book used in Mesopotamia), including the chronicles of Sennacherib, Esarhaddon, and other rulers contemporary with the kings of Israel and Judah. Others contained the Babylonian narratives of the Creation and the Deluge. Subsequent discoveries carried back the proof of the early use of writing far beyond the time of Moses and even of Abraham. American explorers at Nippur in Lower Babylonia discovered thousands of tablets going back to the

third millennium B.C., among which were earlier
narratives of the Creation and Deluge, and lists of
kings and other historical materials. Other excavations, such as those of Woolley at Ur, have amply
confirmed the proof that writing was not only
known but habitually used in Mesopotamia long
before the time when Abraham migrated thence to
Palestine. It was known also, and commonly
used, in the other countries which adjoined
Palestine. From Egypt we have actual manuscripts on papyrus written about 2000 B.C. and
evidence that writing was known a thousand years
earlier or more. A particularly interesting discovery in this connection is that of the Tell el-
Amarna tablets, found in Egypt accidentally by a
peasant woman in 1887, which consist of corre-
spondence between the King of Egypt (Amenhotep
IV, the immediate predecessor of Tutankhamen)
and his officials in Palestine and Syria, written
about the time of the entry of the Israelites under
Joshua into the land of Canaan. We have also
writings from the Hittite Empire in Asia Minor
and from Crete which date from the second
millenium B.C. So though the earliest actual
writing in Hebrew yet discovered is an inscription
found at Byblos in 1926, which some scholars
would date before 1200 B.C., and which is cer-

tainly earlier than 1000 B.C., there is ample evidence that writing was well known in and about Palestine in the time of Moses; and consequently there is no reason to doubt that the authors of the historical books of the Old Testament had written materials (some of which they expressly refer to) on which to base their history of their nation.

But if we agree that the books of the Old Testament were written down between the eighth century and the second before Christ, there is a wide gap between those dates and the earliest copies which we now possess; for it is a surprising fact that the earliest Hebrew manuscript now known of any part of the Bible is not earlier than the ninth century after Christ. The oldest is probably a copy of the Pentateuch in the British Museum, which is believed to be of this date. At Leningrad there is (or was) a copy of the Prophets, which bears the date of A.D. 916. At Oxford there is a copy of nearly the whole Old Testament which is assigned to the tenth century. There are a few which bear dates as early as, or earlier than, these, but these dates are believed (and in some cases known) to be unreliable; and on the whole we must accept the fact that for the Old Testament there is a gap of more than a thousand years between our earliest Hebrew manuscript and the latest of the books contained in it. This need not in itself shake our belief in their general authenticity; for in the case of many of the works of classical literature, which we accept without question, the interval is even greater (see below, p. 33) We can, however, do something to bridge the gap, and also to account for it. The interval with which we have to deal falls into two parts, the dividing-line between which lies about A.D. 100. After the destruction of Jerusalem in A.D. 70, the leaders of the Jewish people, deprived of their country, and threatened by the spread of Christianity, were forced to make their sacred books the centre of their national unity. For this purpose it was felt by them to be necessary to define authoritatively which books were to be regarded as sacred, and to secure, as far as might be, the purity of their text. Accordingly, as there is good reason to believe, about the year 100 a synod of Jews drew up the list of accepted books, as we find it in our Old Testament to-day; those books which we now have in our Apocrypha, which had previously been accepted as almost, if not quite, of equal value, being excluded from it. Further, they prescribed rules to ensure the accurate copying of the sacred text. Copies intended for use in the synagogue were to be written according to precise rules, and

12

with the most minute attention to accuracy. Any copy which was found faulty or damaged was to be destroyed. When a new copy had been made, and its accuracy tested, the old manuscript (especially if it had been in any way damaged) was destroyed or consigned to a lumber-cupboard. This practice accounts for the disappearance of all the early manuscripts, but it is also a guarantee of the accuracy of those that survive. In fact, although even these precise regulations have not sufficed to secure the exact identity of all Hebrew manuscripts, it has brought it about that the differences are of minor character and small importance; and scholars are agreed that the Hebrew books, as we know them to-day, have come down to us without material change since about A.D. 100.

But what about the centuries before this point? For them we have some evidence, though not of a full or conclusive character. In the third century before Christ, when Jews were becoming more and more spread over all parts of the Greek-speaking world, where they habitually spoke Greek and lost the practice of Hebrew, the need arose for a Greek translation of their Scriptures. Such a translation was made in Egypt, where Jews were plentiful in the capital city, Alexandria, and where the interest in literature was lively. It was said to have been promoted by the King himself, Ptolemy Philadelphus, who was engaged in founding his great Library. Now of this translation, commonly known as the Septuagint, or " work of the Seventy," from the number of translators said to have been employed upon it, we have many copies much earlier than the oldest Hebrew manuscript. The great Codex Sinaiticus, of the fourth century, originally had the whole of it, though much had been destroyed before the manuscript left the monastery at Sinai where Tischendorf discovered it. The equally old Codex Vaticanus has practically the whole of it, except the greater part of Genesis; the Codex Alexandrinus, of the fifth century, has the whole of it, apart from a few casual mutilations; and there are many of somewhat later date. But earlier than all these are the Chester Beatty papyri, discovered about 1930, buried in one or more jars in the ruins, probably of a church, in Egypt, and published in a series of parts (1933–7 and 1942). The earliest of these is a copy of the books of Numbers and Deuteronomy, written about A.D. 120–50; from the third century there are large portions of Genesis, Isaiah, Ezekiel, Daniel and Esther, with some smaller fragments of Jeremiah. These are the earliest copies of the Bible as yet known to exist, and they establish our

14

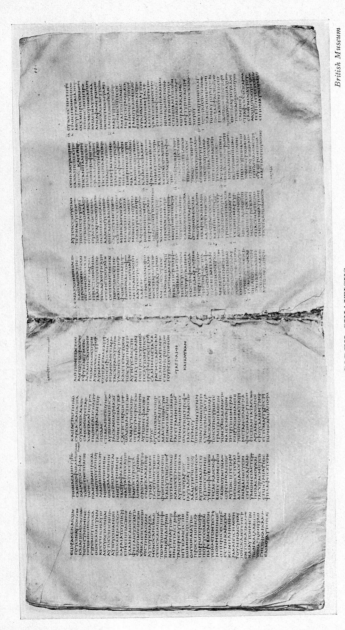

CODEX SINAITICUS

End of St. Luke and beginning of St. John. Fourth Century

PAPYRUS ROLL
Louvre Hyperides

knowledge of this Greek translation of the Hebrew books, made some centuries before the final fixing of the Hebrew text.

Now the Septuagint differs in many, and often not unimportant, details from the Hebrew text. In the first place, it includes those books which were excluded from the Hebrew canon in A.D. 100, and which appear in our Apocrypha. Throughout there are additions, and sometimes omissions, and often varieties of phrasing, which make it clear, either that the Greek translators were working on a Hebrew text differing from that fixed later, or that they took considerable liberties with it. Probably both explanations are true. What is certain is that the Septuagint deserves very careful study, and that the recent discovery of ancient manuscripts of it is an important contribution to our knowledge of the Old Testament.

There is another version of the Hebrew Scriptures which takes us back before the revision of A.D. 100. This is the Samaritan Pentateuch. As we know from 2 Kings xvii. 24-41 and from Josephus, the Samaritans were foreigners imported into the country of the Ten Tribes by the King of Assyria, who there adopted the worship of Jehovah, as the God of the land, but who, when the Jewish leaders refused to let them take part in the rebuilding

15

of the Temple, became bitterly hostile to the Jews.
To them came Manasseh, grandson of a high-priest,
who had been expelled from Jerusalem by Nehemiah because he had married a heathen wife; and
he set up a rival worship at Gerizim, where the
rites of the Samaritan Church are performed to this
day. As their sacred books they had, and still
have, the Pentateuch; and the fact that they recognized these books only is some sign that at the date
of Manasseh's secession (408 B.C.) these were the
only books yet formally accepted by the Jews themselves. The language is Hebrew, but written in
the old characters, not in the square letters adopted
by the Jews shortly before the Christian era. The
Samaritan community is now reduced to a few
score persons living in the town of Nablus; but
they still celebrate their Passover on Mount
Gerizim (it was celebrated in 1935 on April 14),
and they still have manuscripts of their Scriptures,
which they show to favoured travellers (as to the
present writer a few years ago), one of which they
assert to have been written by the great-grandson of
Moses—a claim which the appearance of the
manuscript, though undoubtedly old and worn,
hardly bears out !

The substantial differences between the Samaritan
text and the orthodox Hebrew are not very numer-

16

ous. It is probable that the books of the Penta
teuch, being the first to be recognized as sacred,
were always carefully copied and were not seriously
altered by editors. Still, there are a number of
variations of some interest; and when, as happens
in several instances, the Septuagint version agrees
with the Samaritan, there is strong reason to believe
that they, and not the orthodox Hebrew, represent
the original text.

The general position, therefore, with regard to the
text of the Old Testament is this. It may be
accepted that since about the year A.D. 100 it has
been handed down with no substantial variation;
but before that period it is probable that it had
undergone alterations, not so much in the Pentateuch as in the other books. To recover the original
form we must depend mainly on the Septuagint;
but this can only be done with much caution, for
many of the differences which appear in the Greek
may be, and probably are, due to mistakes, mis-
understandings, or deliberate alterations on the
part of the Greek translators.

Moreover, there was a tendency to alter the
Septuagint text so as to bring it into conformity
with the accepted Hebrew text; a tendency to
which the great Christian scholar, Origen, con-
tributed by producing an edition of the Septuagint

(known as the Hexapla, from its containing six different versions of the text in parallel columns [1]) in which some passages were introduced from the Hebrew, and others marked for omission as not being in the Hebrew. Origen himself carefully marked such passages with special signs ; but copyists tended to omit these. It is therefore no easy task to ascertain the true original form of the Septuagint itself, which is necessary before we can compare it with the Hebrew. Nevertheless it remains a fact that the early manuscripts of the Greek Bible, the Vaticanus, the Sinaiticus, the Alexandrinus, and now the Chester Beatty papyri, are the earliest records which we have of the Old Testament, as they are of the New; and in telling the story of how the New Testament has come down to us, we shall in great measure be telling also the story of the Old.

[A critical edition of the Septuagint on a large scale is in course of publication by the Cambridge University Press, under

---

[1] These six versions were (1) the Hebrew text, (2) the same transliterated into Greek characters, (3) the Greek translation made by Aquila, which follows the official Hebrew very closely, (4) the Greek translation of Symmachus, (5) Origen's edition of the Septuagint, (6) the Greek translation of Theodotion. The versions of Aquila, Symmachus and Theodotion were made in the second century, but have now almost wholly disappeared.

the editorship of A. E. Brooke and N. McLean. Eight parts have appeared, containing Genesis–2 Esdras. In this the text of the best manuscript (Codex Vaticanus where it is extant) is printed with a full apparatus of various readings from other manuscripts and versions. The same text, with a select textual apparatus, is printed in the smaller Cambridge Septuagint, edited by Swete (3 vols., 1887–94). A new handy edition, with a revised text and select textual apparatus, has been published by A. Rahlfs (2 vols., Stuttgart, 1935). The Chester Beatty papyri (enumerated below, pp. 113-8) have now (1946) all been published.]

ADDENDUM (1946). Two interesting discoveries may now be added: (1) Some fragments of Deuteronomy, found in the Rylands Library, written in the second century B.C., and thus the earliest extant Bible MS.; published by C. H. Roberts (1936); (2) a library of clay tablets, discovered by C. F. A. Schaeffer at Ras Shamra in northern Syria, written in a hitherto unknown cuneiform alphabet, and containing religious texts, etc., of the Canaanite kingdom of Ugarit, about 1400–1350 B.C. These, besides throwing much light on the religion of the Canaanites in Palestine at the time of Joshua's invasion, are conclusive evidence of the free use of writing in Palestine at that date.

CHAPTER III

HOW THE BOOKS OF THE NEW TESTAMENT WERE WRITTEN

To understand how the books of the New Testament have come to us, we must know how books were written in the first Christian century. At that time, and during the previous three centuries when the Old Testament was being translated into Greek, books were very different from what they are to-day. Throughout the Græco-Roman world, which included Palestine and Syria, books were written on papyrus, a material made out of the pith of the stems of the papyrus plant, which then grew plentifully in the Nile. This pith was cut into thin strips, which were joined by glue, water and pressure into sheets, which again were fastened together, side by side, so as to form long rolls, on which the writing was inscribed in columns. It is only within our own time that we have come to know much about papyrus books; and this is entirely due to the discoveries that have been made in Egypt. Papyrus, though it must have been fairly strong when new, is a delicate material. It is easily destroyed by damp, and when dry tends

20

to become very brittle. Consequently, with the exception of some charred rolls found in the ruins of Herculaneum, which was buried by the great eruption of Vesuvius in A.D. 79, no papyrus books have survived save in Egypt, where the soil is so dry that even fragile objects, when once buried in the sands, may be preserved for centuries.[1] It is from the graves and ruins and rubbish-heaps of Egypt that writings on papyrus have been restored to us in great numbers. Papyrus rolls in the Egyptian language, written in hieroglyphs or in later forms of writing, have been found which date back to about 2000 B.C.; and rolls written in Greek dating from about 300 B.C., when, after the conquest of Egypt by Alexander, Greeks settled in the country in considerable numbers.

The first Greek papyrus to be discovered in Egypt came to light in 1778. It was a non-literary document of no great importance, the only one left of a packet of about fifty, the others having been burnt by the natives (as they said) for the sake of their smell. Other finds were made sporadically in the course of the next century, including some rolls of Homer, and (a welcome foretaste of what

---

[1] Quite recently it has been announced that some papyri have been found in the desert to the south of Palestine, where the conditions are similar.

was to come) four of the lost speeches of the great Athenian orator Hyperides. But the real period of papyrus discovery began in 1877, when a great number of documents were unearthed in the Fayum, a province lying to the west of the Nile, where, as we now know, there were many Greek settlements. Most of these were not literary, but in 1890 the British Museum acquired a most valuable group of literary papyri, including the lost history of the Constitution of Athens by Aristotle, and the previously unknown Mimes (or short dramatic sketches) of Herodas. In 1894 began the great series of discoveries of papyri, chiefly from excavations on the site of the ancient city of Oxyrhynchus, made by Grenfell and Hunt. From this time forward the search for papyri in Egypt has gone on without a break, and a constant stream of texts has flowed into the libraries of Europe and America, so that we now have many thousands of non-literary documents and several hundreds of literary texts— most of them, it is true, only small fragments from rubbish heaps, but including a substantial number of rolls of some length, which have given us an assured knowledge of the methods of book production from about 300 B.C. to the Arab conquest of Egypt in A.D. 640. Latest among these, and most important for our present purpose, is the

22

recent discovery of the group of Biblical texts known as the Chester Beatty Biblical Papyri, of which much more will have to be said.

We now know that the normal form of book, from the great days of the classical literature of Greece to the beginning of the fourth century after Christ, was the papyrus roll. The roll might be of various dimensions, according to need, but practical convenience dictated that it should not be more than 30 to 35 feet long—a length which was sufficient for a single book of Thucydides or a single Gospel. The height might vary from about 5 inches for a pocket volume of poetry to 15 inches for a register of taxes; but a normal height for a work of literature was about 10 inches. The writing was arranged in columns, which for poetry would be regulated by the length of a line of verse, but for prose were generally between $2\frac{1}{2}$ and $3\frac{1}{2}$ inches wide. There would be narrow intervals (usually about half an inch) between the columns, and wider margins at top and bottom, where words accidentally omitted would sometimes be inserted. There was normally no ornamentation, no separation of words, and very little punctuation. It is very odd that this should have been so, since it must have added to the difficulty of reading quickly, and increased the probability of misunderstanding through a wrong division of words. Also it must have occasioned a good deal of difficulty in the verifying of quotations, and encouraged a writer to quote from memory rather than take the trouble to look up a passage in a roll. Yet this habit continued throughout the classical period, and it is a fact that with practice the non-separation of words does not occasion great difficulty, but only occasional hesitation. Certain it is that the separation of words only came in gradually during the Middle Ages, first for Latin and later for Greek; and that punctuation continued to be casual and incomplete until after the invention of printing.

Until quite recently it has been supposed that the papyrus roll continued in general use for books until the early part of the fourth century, when it was superseded by the vellum codex[1], or modern book form of sheets and pages. Vellum, a material prepared from the skins of calves, sheep, and other animals, was adopted as a writing material about the beginning of the second century B.C., by king Eumenes of Pergamum in Asia Minor, who was ambitious of forming a library, but was unable to obtain papyrus because his rival, Ptolemy of Egypt, refused to allow the export of it. From Pergamum the new material received the name of

[1] See footnote, p. 145.

pergamené, which is the origin of our word *parchment.*
Apart, however, from this particular occasion (and
we do not know how long the embargo on the
export of papyrus lasted, nor how effective it
could have been, since it was still exported to
Rome and elsewhere), the papyrus roll continued
to be predominant, and vellum was in general
only used for note-books and cheap copies until
the end of the third century after Christ. Then
its superior advantages seem to have been suddenly
realized. It was more durable (while, as said
above, all papyrus manuscripts have perished
except in Egypt, thousands and thousands of
vellum manuscripts have survived); it provided a
beautiful surface for writing; and, arranged in
sheets and pages, it could contain in a single
volume a far greater quantity of matter than the
papyrus roll. It became possible to have the whole
of Homer or Virgil or of the Bible in a single
volume, instead of in a number of distinct rolls,
which might easily become disarranged or separated. From this point the vellum codex definitely
superseded the papyrus roll, and so continued until
the invention of paper and printing, at the end of
the Middle Ages.

Now this event is of great importance for the
history of the Bible, because it happened just at the

time when the Emperor Constantine accepted Christianity as the official religion of the Roman Empire (about A.D. 313–25). Only a few years before, Christianity had been an unrecognized and often a persecuted religion; and we know that in the great persecutions of Decius (A.D. 249–51) and Diocletian (A.D. 303–5) many copies of the Christian books were destroyed. Now it was officially recognized, and we know that one of Constantine's first acts was to order fifty copies of the Greek Bible to be written on vellum for his capital, Constantinople. All through the empire there must have been a similar demand for copies of the Scriptures, and a great stimulus must have been given to their production. It is just to this period that the great codices which we still possess, the Vaticanus and the Sinaiticus, belong; and from that time we have quantities of vellum manuscripts which carry us through the Middle Ages, down to the invention of printing.

In papyrus manuscripts the writing is generally in rather small letters, for the most part separately formed, but with occasional links between them. On vellum it is in large capitals, quite distinct, a type of writing known as *uncial*. This is a very handsome form, and the early uncials, such as the Sinaiticus and Alexandrinus, are among the finest

26

books in existence; but it involved the use of very large volumes. The Sinaiticus, when complete, must have consisted of about 720 leaves, or 1,440 pages, measuring 15 by $13\frac{1}{2}$ inches; the Vaticanus of about 820 of $10\frac{1}{2}$ by 10 inches; the Alexandrinus, of about 820 of $12\frac{1}{2}$ by $10\frac{1}{2}$ inches. These would serve well for reading in church or for study in a library, but were not handy for personal use; so in the ninth century a new form of writing was developed out of the handwriting in common use, with small letters linked together, and hence called *minuscule* or *cursive*. This quickly superseded the more cumbrous uncial, and from the tenth century to the fifteenth century practically all manuscripts were so written. It is to this class that the great majority of the surviving manuscripts of the Greek Bible belong. While there are about 200 uncial manuscripts of the New Testament known, of which all but some sixty are mere fragments, the minuscules are over 4,000 in number.

Until quite lately it was supposed that there was no intermediate stage between the papyrus roll and the vellum codex; but the discovery of the Chester Beatty papyri has proved, what was beginning to be suspected before, that such an intermediate stage did exist, when the papyrus material was combined

27

with the codex form, and that this stage was of particular importance for the Christian Scriptures. The first inkling of this was given by a fragment found at Oxyrhynchus and published in 1899, which contained on one sheet portions of the first and last chapters of St. John, showing that they were the outer leaves of a quire which must have contained between them all the rest of the Gospel. Calculation showed that this implied that the whole Gospel was written in a single quire of 50 leaves or 100 pages—a rather inconvenient form of book, one would think, but of which other examples came to light from time to time. As these discoveries of papyrus codices multiplied, it was observed that the majority of them were of Christian literature. It became clear that in the third century, while the papyrus roll was still the dominant form of book for pagan literature, most of the Christian literature was written in codices. Sometimes these were single-quire volumes, like the St. John just mentioned, while some were formed of a number of quires of 8 or 10 or 12 leaves, more like a modern book. The final proof was given by the Chester Beatty papyri, which are a group of papyrus codices of various books of the Bible, mostly of the third century, but in at least one instance going back to the second century, and even to the first

PAPYRUS CODEX

Ezekiel and Esther (Chester Beatty Papyrus IX)

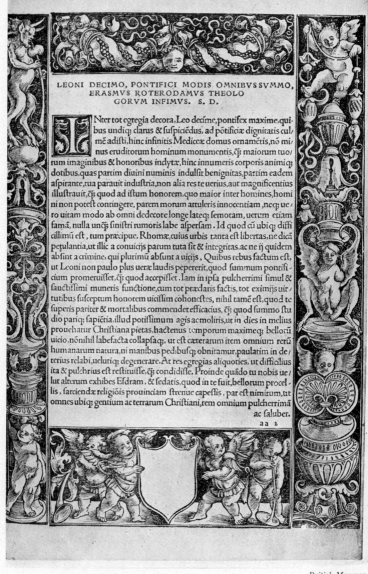

LEONI DECIMO, PONTIFICI MODIS OMNIBVS SVMMO,
ERASMVS ROTERODAMVS THEOLO
GORVM INFIMVS. S. D.

Nter tot egregia decora, Leo decíme, pontifex maxime, qui
bus undiq; clarus & suspiciédus, ad pótificiæ dignitatis cul
mé adisti, hinc infinitis Mediceæ domus ornamétis, nó mi
nus eruditorum hominum monumentis, cq; maiorum tuo/
rum imaginibus & honoribus indytæ, hinc innumeris corporis animiq;
dotibus, quas partim diuini numinis indulsit benignitas, partim eadem
aspirante, tua parauit industria, non alia res te uerius, aut magnificentius
illustrauit, cq; quod ad istum honorem, quo maior inter homines, homi
ni non potest contingere, parem morum attuleris innocentiam, neq; ue/
ro uitam modo ab omni dedecore longe lateq; semotam, uerum etiam
famâ, nulla unq; sinistri rumoris labe aspersam. Id quod cû undiq; diffi
cillimû est, tum præcipue, Rhomæ, cuius urbis tanta est libertas, ne dicâ
petulantia, ut illic a conuícijs parum tuta sit & integritas, ac ne ñ quidem
absint a crimine, qui plurimû absunt a uicijs. Quibus rebus factum est,
ut Leoni non paulo plus ueræ laudis pepererit, quod summum pontifi
cium promeruisset, cq; quod accepisset. Iam in ipsa pulcherrimi simul &
sanctissimi muneris functione, cum tot præclaris factis, tot eximijs uir/
tutibus susceptum honorem uicissim cohonestes, nihil tamé est, quod te
superis pariter & mortalibus commendet efficacius, cq; quod summo stu
dio pariq; sapiétia, illud potissimum agis ac moliris, ut in dies in melius
prouehatur Christiana pietas, hactenus temporum maximeq; belloru̅
uicio, nónihil labefacta collapsaq;, ut est cæterarum item omnium reru̅
humanarum natura, ni manibus pedibusq; obnitamur, paulatim in de/
terius relabi, uelutiq; degenerare. At res egregias aliquoties, ut difficilius
ita & pulchrius est restituisse, cq; condidisse. Proinde quâdo tu nobis ue/
lut alterum exhibes Esdram, & sedatis, quod in te fuit, bellorum procel/
lis, sarciendæ religiôis prouinciam strenue capessis, par est nimirum, ut
omnes ubiq; gentium ac terrarum Christiani, rem omnium pulcherrimâ
ac saluber.

a a 2

A PAGE FROM ERASMUS'S EDITION OF THE NEW TESTAMENT, 1516

[29]

half of it. It now seems clear that the Christian community, realizing the advantage of a form of book which could contain more than a single Gospel, adopted (if they did not actually invent) the codex form, in which several books could be combined. Thus one of the Chester Beatty papyri, of the first half of the third century, contained when complete all four Gospels and the Acts; another, which is at least as early and may be of the end of the second century, contained all the epistles of St. Paul; another contained the books of Ezekiel, Daniel and Esther. Some of these codices are formed of single quires, running to as many as 118 leaves, formed of 59 sheets of papyrus laid one upon another and folded in the middle; one (the Gospels and Acts) goes to the other extreme, being composed of a succession of quires of only two leaves; others have quires of 10 or 12 leaves. On the whole it seems probable that the earliest experiments in the use of the codex took the form of single-quire volumes or of quires of two leaves, but that it came to be realized that quires of 8–12 leaves were more convenient, and these were used in the later papyrus codices, as they were in the vellum codices and eventually in our modern paper printed books.

We are now in a position to picture to ourselves

how the books of the New Testament were first written and circulated. The shorter Epistles, such as the second and third of St. John, or St. Paul's letter to Philemon, would have been written on a single sheet of papyrus, like the ordinary private letters of which many examples have been found. They would have been folded up, fastened with a thread secured by a clay seal, and sent by hand to their destination. The longer Epistles would have occupied rolls of various lengths, from about 3 to 4 feet for Philippians or Colossians to about 15 feet in the case of Romans. The longest books, Matthew, Luke and Acts, would each have required a roll of from 30 to 35 feet, and the shorter ones, Mark, John, and Revelation, proportionately less. Each book and each Epistle originally circulated separately. Copies would be made and sent to other churches, as Paul asked that the Epistle to the Colossians should be sent to the church at Laodicea. It would be only gradually, if at all, that any one church would secure a complete set of all the books. Some Gospels would be more popular than others; there is reason to believe that Mark, which is shorter and contains less of our Lord's teaching, circulated less than Matthew and Luke. The book of Revelation was not accepted by all churches, and the authenticity of 2 Peter

30

was questioned by some. On the other hand, some books which did not eventually secure acceptance in the authoritative Canon of Scripture were at first regarded with almost equal respect, and were even included in the great fourth-century codices. Thus the Codex Sinaiticus includes the 4th book of Maccabees, the Epistle of Barnabas and the " Shepherd " of Hermas. The Alexandrinus has 3 and 4 Maccabees at the end of the Old Testament, and the two Epistles of Clement, and originally also the Psalms of Solomon, at the end of the New. The church to which the Chester Beatty collection belonged had a copy of the Book of Enoch. A group of churches in Syria in the second century for some time read a Gospel which passed under the name of St. Peter, until a bishop perceived that it was not authentic; part of it was discovered in 1892 in a vellum codex, probably of the sixth century, dug up in Egypt, which contained also parts of Enoch and of the Apocalypse of Peter. In Syria also the four Gospels were to a considerable extent replaced by a Harmony of the Four Gospels (known as the *Diatessaron*), compiled by Tatian about A.D. 170; of this, which was supposed to survive only in Arabic and Armenian translations, a small Greek fragment was found a few years ago as far away as the ruins of a Roman fort on the Euphrates, and has lately been published.[1] A fuller account is given of this later.

There was thus, for the first century or so after the earliest Christian books were written, much irregularity in the way they circulated, and some uncertainty as to which were to be regarded as authoritative. But in the course of the second century after Christ the four Gospels which we know singled themselves out above all the other narratives which St. Luke in the preface to his Gospel tells us were in existence in his time, and were accepted as the pre-eminently authentic records of our Lord's life. By the end of that century we find Irenæus asserting that four was the obviously right number of Gospels, analogous to the four winds or the four quarters of the world or the four cherubim. It now seems possible (what was formerly regarded as impossible) that he may have been accustomed to see the four Gospels united in a single codex. The Chester Beatty papyri have given us an actual example of such a codex from the early part of the third century; and as they also include a codex of the early second century (of the books of Numbers and Deuteronomy), it is quite possible that the Gospels also circulated in this form before his time. This

[1] By C. Kraeling, in K. and S. Lake's *Studies and Documents*, No. III (London, 1935).

would make it easier for them to be marked out as separate from, and superior to, all other narratives.

What was happening to the text of the books during this period, and how far they were being copied accurately, is another question, to which we shall return; but meanwhile it may be useful to point out how immensely greater is our evidence for the text of the New Testament books than for any other ancient book. We have already explained that the lack of durability of the material on which they were written (papyrus) accounts for the total disappearance, apart from such fragments on papyrus as have recently been discovered in Egypt, of all manuscripts earlier than the fourth century. For all the works of classical antiquity we have to depend on manuscripts written long after their original composition. The author who is in best case in this respect is Virgil; yet the earliest manuscript of Virgil that we now possess was written some 350 years after his death. For all other classical writers, the interval between the date of the author and the earliest extant manuscript of his works is much greater. For Livy it is about 500 years, for Horace 900, for most of Plato 1,300, for Euripides 1,600. On the other hand, the great vellum uncials of the New Testament were written perhaps some 250 years after the date when the

Gospels were actually composed, while we now have papyrus manuscripts which reduce the interval by a hundred years. And while the manuscripts of any classical author amount at most to a few score, and in some cases only to a few units, the manuscripts of the Bible are reckoned by thousands. Their very quantity adds to the difficulties of an editor, since the more the manuscripts, the greater the number of various readings; but they make the authenticity of the works themselves overwhelmingly certain.

There is also another kind of evidence, the importance of which will appear later, but which must be briefly mentioned here, because it belongs to the period with which we are now dealing. During these early centuries, before Christianity was recognized by Constantine, the Christian Scriptures were not only being copied in their original Greek; they were also being translated into other tongues. As Christianity spread outwards from Palestine, through Syria, through Asia Minor, Italy, Roman Africa and Egypt, and converts were made not only among Greek-speaking Jews but among communities to whom Greek was less familiar, a demand grew up for the Scriptures in other languages. The three earliest, and therefore the most important for our purpose, were in the

34

principal languages of the adjoining peoples—
Syriac, Latin and Coptic (the language of the
natives of Egypt). It is only lately that we have
learnt much about the first versions in these
tongues; for in each case the early version was
eventually superseded by another, which became
the accepted Bible of that people, and of the earlier
translations relatively few manuscripts have survived, and most of these are only fragments. But
it now seems certain that the books of the New
Testament were translated into all these languages
before the end of the third century, while the Syriac
and Latin almost certainly go back to the second.
The original translators must have used Greek
manuscripts then existing; so that, so far as we
can ascertain the original form of these various
versions (itself not an easy task), we have the
evidence of Greek manuscripts earlier than any
which have come down to us. Further, these
translations show us what kind of text was in use
in the countries in which they were produced.

If therefore we look back over the earliest generations of Christianity, from the time of our Lord to
the date (somewhere about A.D. 325) when
Christianity became the accepted religion of the
Roman Empire, we see first of all a period of some
forty years when the narrative of our Lord's life

and teaching circulated orally, in the preaching of His disciples, or in written records which have not come down to us; and when St. Paul was writing his letters to various Christian churches which he and his companions had founded. Then, about the years 65 to 75, we have the composition of what are known as the three Synoptic Gospels, Mark, Luke and Matthew, Mark's being the earliest, and Matthew and Luke using him and also other narratives and collections of sayings. The Book of Acts belongs to the same period, being the second part of Luke's history. Revelation is now generally assigned to the time of the persecution of Domitian, about A.D. 95; and St. John's Gospel also must be late in the century. Then we have a period of rather over two hundred years, when the various books circulated, either singly in separate papyrus rolls or combined into small groups in papyrus codices, with no central control to ensure a uniform text, but rather exposed to indefinite variation at the hands of local scribes, and perhaps assuming a somewhat different character in different parts of the world. During this period also translations were made into Syriac, Latin and Coptic. Meanwhile Christianity was from time to time exposed to persecutions by the Roman emperors and governors, when copies of the Scriptures were a special object of search and destruction, which increased the difficulty of securing an accurate transmission of the text. Many churches must have been dependent on copies locally made by inexperienced scribes; and though scholars or bishops may from time to time have tried to secure and circulate more correct copies, their efforts would probably have effect only in their own neighbourhood. It is a period of confusion, when people were thinking only of the substance of the Christian teaching, and caring little for the verbal accuracy of the text; and when there were no great libraries, as there were for pagan literature, in which the books could be carefully copied and revised by skilled scholars. It is by realizing the conditions in which Christians lived in these earliest centuries that we can best understand the problems presented to us with regard to the text of the Greek Bible.

CHAPTER IV

FROM MANUSCRIPT TO PRINT

FROM the description given in the last chapter of the conditions of the earliest Christian generations, it will be easy to understand what a change was produced by the acceptance of Christianity by Constantine, and the simultaneous adoption of the vellum codex as the standard form of book. The peril of the destruction of the sacred books by persecutors was over. A great demand arose for copies to be placed in Churches throughout the Empire. It was possible for scholars to set themselves to compare the many divergent manuscripts, to settle what seemed to them the most correct form of text, and to have it multiplied and circulated. The new writing material made it possible to include all the accepted books of both Testaments in a single volume. The very conception of a New Testament, to set beside the Old Testament of the Jewish Scriptures, only finally took form now. From this time forward there was no danger of any serious corruption of the Scriptures. All that took place was a certain progressive editing of them, involving slight verbal variations for the sake of greater clearness, or harmonizing different versions of the same narrative, or substituting conventional phrases for those less familiar. In this way an accepted text gradually came into being, which spread over the whole Greek-speaking world. We cannot assign a precise date to it. There is no record of any authoritative revision of the text at any given moment, comparable to the work of the committees who produced our Authorised and Revised Versions. All we can say is that, as the result of a process which went on from the fourth century to about the eighth, a standard type of text was produced, which is found in the vast majority of the manuscripts that have come down to us. At least ninety-six per cent of the extant manuscripts of the Greek New Testament are later than the eighth century; and of these only a handful preserve traces of the other types of text which were in existence before the adoption of the standard text, and out of which it was created. This standard ecclesiastical text is generally known as the Byzantine text (from the ancient name of Constantinople, the capital of the Greek-speaking world), or, more commonly, as the

39

Received Text. It does not differ in substance from the earlier types; no Christian truth or doctrine is affected by the differences; but the verbal differences are numerous. They are the result of gradual editorial revision of earlier manuscripts; and it is the task of scholarship to try to get behind it to the earlier texts, and as near as may be to the words which the original writers used.

We can now therefore proceed more quickly with the story of how the Bible text was transmitted to us, and by what means and by what discoveries we have been able to recover, at any rate in great measure, the text which the lapse of time had obscured. From the fourth century to the ninth, the Bible circulated in manuscripts in the large uncial writing which we have described above; but when the more convenient minuscule writing came into use, the cumbrous old volumes were set aside and disappeared. Only a few score of them survived at all, and most of these were hidden from public view, and have only come to light as the result of zealous search, which will be described later, in quite modern times. Meanwhile, in other parts of the Christian world, the Scriptures were similarly being handed down in translations. The early versions of which we have already spoken were superseded by revisions or

40

new translations: the old Latin by the Vulgate of St. Jerome (A.D. 382–404), which was the Bible of the Western world throughout the Middle Ages and is still the Bible of the Roman Church; the old Syriac by the Peshitta of Bishop Rabbula (about A.D. 411); and the old Coptic version of Upper Egypt (Sahidic) by a version in the Bohairic dialect of Lower Egypt. Other translations were made into Ethiopic, Armenian, Georgian, Arabic, Gothic, with which we need not concern ourselves, though scholars make some use of their evidence.

From the ninth century to the fifteenth the same process goes on, the Scriptures still being multiplied in thousands of copies by hand, and the older copies tending to be worn out, damaged or lost, and each generation producing its own fresh crop, but now in the smaller minuscule hand (whether Greek or Latin) and in volumes of more portable size. And so we come to the moment when, in the middle of the fifteenth century, everything was revolutionized by the invention of printing. Seldom can two such epoch-making events have occurred in consecutive years as happened then. In 1453 the Turks stormed Constantinople and finally destroyed the Greek Empire, driving out Greek scholars, who carried the knowledge of Greek language and literature to the western world; and in 1454 the first document known to us appeared from the printing press at Mainz. The former made the more sensation at the time, and its consequences affect us still; but the latter had the more revolutionary results for the human race, and, among other things, for the history of the Bible.

Printing first made its appearance in Europe in single-sheet *indulgences,* issued nominally as a means of raising money for the war against the Turks; but the first complete printed book was, appropriately enough, the Bible. Not, however, a Greek Bible, but the Latin Vulgate, which was the Bible as generally known to the western world. It is a stately folio volume, commonly known (from the fact that the copy which first attracted the attention of scholars was in the library of Cardinal Mazarin at Paris) as the Mazarin Bible. King George III's copy of it may be seen any day in the King's Library at the British Museum. It was printed by the German printers, Gutenberg and Fust, at Mainz, and is known to have been in circulation by August, 1456. It was a wonderful achievement of the infant art, and copies of it are highly prized. About forty copies are known to exist, all now in public libraries. The last to come into the market was bought a few years ago by

42

the Congress of the United States for the national
library at Washington for about £60,000. If that
was a fair market price for a printed Bible, of
which many other copies existed, and of no
textual importance, the £100,000 paid for the
unique Codex Sinaiticus, more than 1,100 years
older and one of the most valuable witnesses to
the text of the Bible, seems a very good bargain.

It was sixty years later that the first Greek Bible
made its appearance. The credit for producing
it ought to have fallen to Cardinal Ximenes,
Archbishop of Toledo. As early as 1502 he
began to prepare an edition of the entire Greek
Bible in the University of Alcala, and not of the
Greek text alone, but accompanied by the Hebrew
in the Old Testament and the Latin throughout.
Such a large undertaking necessarily progressed
slowly. The New Testament, which was the first
to be printed, was ready by the beginning of 1514,
but it was held back from publication until the
Old Testament should be completed. This was
not until the middle of 1517, and even then publication was delayed for some unknown reason;
so that it was not until 1522 that the Complutensian Polyglot (so called from Complutum, the
Latin name of Alcala, where the work was done)
was actually given to the world. Meanwhile a

publisher at Basle, Froben by name, had heard of the work in progress, and determined to anticipate it. Accordingly he commissioned Erasmus, the foremost scholar of the Reformation, to prepare an edition of the Greek New Testament, and urged on him the utmost speed. Erasmus, who had for some time been anxious to undertake an edition of the Greek New Testament, readily accepted the commission. Using such manuscripts as happened to be available at Basle (two of them lent by Dean Colet from the library of St. Paul's), he set to work in September, 1515, and in March, 1516, his edition was published, thus reaching the world six years earlier than the work of Ximenes, and in a much handier and cheaper form.

It was a great service to scholarship and religion to make the New Testament known in its original language; but Erasmus's hurried work was far from being satisfactory, even with regard to the materials then available, and still less from the point of view of modern scholarship with its vastly increased resources. He had consulted only a handful of manuscripts, mostly of quite late date. For the Gospels he used mainly a single manuscript of the fifteenth century. For Revelation the one manuscript he used was defective at the end, and Erasmus supplied the last six verses by a translation from the Latin into his own imperfect Greek. Nevertheless his edition became the basis of the Greek text in universal use down to our own day. It was from the text of Erasmus that the first English version of the Greek was translated, as will be described shortly; and the continental printers who produced other editions of the Greek New Testament all took Erasmus as their foundation. Erasmus himself produced five more editions, and in that of 1527, which was his definitive edition, he made some use of the Complutensian; but the general inadequacy of the foundation of the work remained unaffected.

Among the numerous editions which followed that of Erasmus in the sixteenth century, only one need be mentioned, namely that produced by the French printer Robert Estienne, or Stephanus, in 1550. This is important, because it is this text which (with very slight alterations) continued to be reprinted for the next three hundred years, and is still to be found in our ordinary Greek Testaments. It is with this that the texts produced by modern scholarship have to be compared, and if the measure of the advance is to be appreciated, it is essential to understand how very slender were the resources at the disposal of the editor of 1550 compared with those at our service to-day.

45

Stephanus used mainly the text of Erasmus, but revised it to some extent from the Complutensian edition and from fifteen manuscripts to which he had access in Paris. One of these was really old, that which is now known as the Codex Bezæ, but for reasons which will appear later little use was made of it. The rest were all late manuscripts, from the tenth to the fifteenth century. They represent only the standard Byzantine text; the much earlier witnesses which have since come to light were not available then, and no one thought of searching for them. It was sufficient for Bible students that they had the Bible in Greek; it did not yet occur to them to ask whether the text was the most correct obtainable.

CHAPTER V

THE ENGLISH BIBLE

THE Reformation produced a great demand for translations of the Bible into the languages of the peoples of Western Europe; for the Reformers found one of their chief weapons for their campaign against Rome in placing the Scriptures in the hands of the common people. We come therefore now to the genesis of our English Bible.

In pre-Reformation days the Bible had been translated into English, at first in separate books from the time of Bede (d. 735) onwards, but completely only by Wyclif and his colleagues in 1382–8. These versions, however, were all made from the Latin Vulgate, and have had no influence on our present English Bible. The true father of this is William Tyndale, who on the publication of the Greek New Testament by Erasmus was filled with the resolve to translate it into English, so that, as he said, the boy that drove the plough might know the Scriptures. He

47

had hoped to secure for this the patronage of the Bishop of London, Tunstall, who was a friend of Erasmus; but finding no encouragement there, nor anywhere in England, he migrated in 1524 to Hamburg, and there completed his work. In 1525 he began printing it at Cologne, and being driven thence by enemies of the Reformation, he finished it at Worms, and thence copies reached England early in 1526. It was vigorously condemned by the authorities of Church and State, who attributed to error many novelties which were in fact due to Tyndale's use of the original Greek, whereas they themselves were only acquainted with the Latin; but the public appetite was whetted, and before long, as the Reformation made progress in England, the demand for an English Bible became irresistible.

Tyndale himself, before his martyrdom at the hands of the Imperial authorities in 1536, had revised his New Testament in 1534 and 1535, had published (in 1530) the Pentateuch, translated from the original Hebrew, and had translated, but not published, the historical books of the Old Testament. This work was never accepted by the rulers of the Church in England; yet before his death a complete English Bible had been published, in which his translation was incorporated. This was the work of his disciple,

48

TITLE-PAGE TO PART I FROM COVERDALE'S TRANSLATION
OF THE BIBLE, 1535

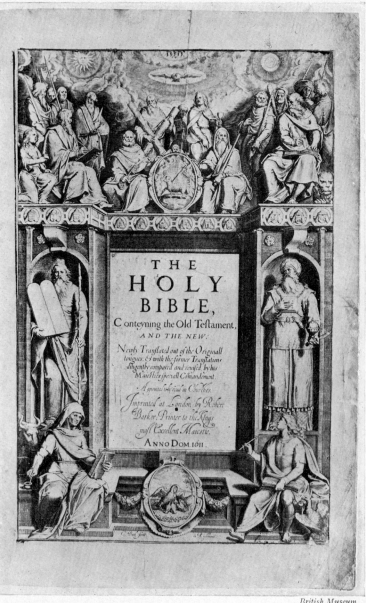

THE
HOLY
BIBLE,
Conteyning the Old Testament,
AND THE NEW:

Newly Translated out of the Originall
tongues: & with the former Translations
diligently compared and reuised, by his
Maiesties speciall Comandement

Appointed to be read in Churches.

Imprinted at London by Robert
Barker, Printer to the Kings
most Excellent Maiestie.

ANNO DOM. 1611.

TITLE-PAGE TO KING JAMES'S, OR THE AUTHORISED VERSION, 1611

Miles Coverdale, who had the patronage of Thomas Cromwell, then chief minister of Henry VIII. Utilizing Tyndale's version, and completing it by a translation of his own from German and Latin Bibles, he was able to produce his work by the end of 1535; so that about Christmas in 1935 we could commemorate the fourth centenary of the first complete English printed Bible. This edition was dedicated to Henry VIII, who had now quarrelled with the Roman Church; and a second edition in 1537 was definitely licensed by the King. From this moment Englishmen possessed, and were allowed to possess, an English Bible.

There follows a period of some seventy-five years, during which the work of revising and improving the English Bible was almost continually in progress. Throughout, the work of Tyndale formed the foundation, and more than anyone else he established the rhythms and furnished much of the language which is familiar to us in the Authorised Version. In 1537 Cromwell and Cranmer co-operated in the production of a Bible (known as " Matthew's ") which silently incorporated Tyndale's unpublished version of the historical books of the Old Testament; but this was superseded in 1539 by a further revision by

Coverdale, known as the Great Bible. This was the first Bible to be formally authorized for public use; for an injunction was issued by Cromwell requiring a copy to be set up in every parish church. A contemporary chronicler paints a vivid picture of the crowds that gathered round the six copies which were set up in various parts of St. Paul's, listening to those who read aloud from them even to the disturbance of the regular services. In two years seven editions were called for; and though a change in Henry's policy then caused him to discourage Protestantism, the English people had now become definitely Bible-minded. During the reign of Edward VI editions of Tyndale, Coverdale, and the Great Bible poured from the press; and when Mary's accession put an end to this, the work was carried on by the Protestant exiles, who at Geneva produced, first a New Testament (1557) and then a complete Bible (1560), with notes in a strongly Calvinistic tone, and of a popular character. All previous Bibles had been large in form, suitable for use in Churches, and printed in "black letter"; but the Geneva Bible was issued in smaller forms, suitable for personal and domestic use, and for the first time was printed in roman type, and with the division into verses, first made by Stephanus for the Greek New Testament in 1551.[1] With the accession of Elizabeth the Bible in this form rapidly spread from the churches to the homes; and though a new revision was prepared in 1568 by the bishops (whence it is known as the Bishops' Bible), this was mainly for use in churches, and the Geneva Bible remained the Bible of the people until it was superseded by the Authorised Version of 1611. A rival version by English Roman Catholic refugees (New Testament at Rheims in 1582, the whole Bible at Douai in 1609) had little effect, though it was utilized by the authors of the Authorised Version.

The Authorised Version may be put down as the best deed ever done by James I. It was he that seized upon the idea when it was put forward by Dr. Reynolds, the Puritan leader, at the Hampton Court Conference of 1604; it was he that suggested that the work of revision should be entrusted to the universities; it was he that insisted that it should not be encumbered or prejudiced by any notes, and so preserved it from

[1] The Hebrew Old Testament was divided into verses by Rabbi Nathan in 1448 (first printed in a Venice edition of 1524). This division was adopted in the Latin Bible of Pagninus in 1528, with a different division in the N.T. The first Bible that has the present verse division in both Testaments is Stephanus' Vulgate of 1555.

having any party colour. The work was divided among six companies, two in London and two each at Oxford and Cambridge. It was taken in hand in 1607, and in two years the companies had completed their first draft. A smaller committee, composed of two representatives from each company, then revised the draft in nine months, after which it was seen through the press by two editors, Dr. Miles Smith (who wrote the excellent preface) and Bishop Bilson. And so, in 1611, the great English Bible appeared. It was the result of 86 years' gestation, with Tyndale's work, as supplemented by Coverdale, always at the base of it; and the result was final. Though revisions had been so frequent previously, no one proposed to revise the version of 1611 for two hundred and seventy years. Though the Geneva Bible was pre-eminently the Bible of the Puritans, and the Puritans were in ascendancy until 1660, the Authorised Version drove it out of the field by sheer merit. The last Geneva Bible was printed in 1644. It is strange that a version of such outstanding merit and success should be the work of a committee; for committees are not generally happy in drafting literary prose. It may be attributed in part to the strong imprint given by the genius of Tyndale, in part to the good sense of the revisers in avoiding unnecessary and pedantic alterations; and in part to the ingrained aptitude for nobility of phrase characteristic of Tudor and Jacobean England.

The misfortune of the version, for which the revisers were not to blame, was that they had such a defective text to translate from. Tyndale and Coverdale worked on Erasmus's text, aided by German and Latin translations. The Genevans and King James's revisers had the "received text" of 1550. All alike were in fact accepting as the authentic Greek text the form which it had assumed after 1,400 years of transmission by manuscript, and with the deterioration, small in each detail but cumulatively great, due to the errors of scribes and the well-meant efforts of editors. For the moment, however, the work was done, and admirably done. The English people had received a version as good as the scholarship of the day could produce from the available materials, and incomparably superior in literary merit to any translation into any other language. It is the simple truth that, as literature, the English Authorised Version is superior to the original Greek. It was the good fortune of the English nation that its Bible was produced at a time when the genius of the language for noble prose was at its height, and when a natural sense of ſtyle was not infected by self-conscious scholarship. The beauty of the language commended the teaching of the sacred books and made them dear to the heart of the people, while it made an indelible and enduring impression alike on literature and on popular speech.

The work of bringing the Bible to the people was now done. It remained for scholars to amend the text upon which the translators had worked, and to reſtore, as nearly as might be, the Greek text to the form in which it was originally written by its authors. That was to be the task of the next three hundred years, and remains our task to-day.

CHAPTER VI

THE SEARCH FOR MANUSCRIPTS

BY 1611 the Western world had got its Bible in Greek and England had got its Bible in English. It might seem that the work was done; but a new work now had to be begun. As has been shown, the Greek Bible had been printed from the first manuscripts that came to hand, and from this text the English Bible had been translated. As it happened, the Greek Old Testament was in better state than the New, since Pope Sixtus V had caused, in 1587, the production of an edition of the Septuagint mainly based on the great Vatican MS., which was and still is the best single authority for it, and this text was frequently reprinted; but Erasmus's New Testament, which with little change had become the " received text," was taken from a few late manuscripts. For two hundred and fifty years, and to a great extent even to-day, this Greek text and this English Bible remained in possession of the field, and few people realized that they were not wholly satisfactory. It needed three centuries of work to collect the materials necessary for their improvement, to digest the results, and to set them before the world at large. That has been the work on which the scholars of Europe and America have been engaged; and in it English scholars have taken an honourable, and often the leading, part.

The first impulse, indeed, came from England, only sixteen years after the publication of the Authorised Version, when the great Codex Alexandrinus came to this country. It was a gift from Cyril Lucar, Patriarch of Constantinople, offered through Sir Thomas Roe, British Ambassador to the Porte, to James I, but did not actually reach England till 1627, when Charles I was on the throne. It is a manuscript of great antiquity, written, as scholars are generally agreed, in the first half of the fifth century, probably in Egypt. Cyril had been Patriarch of Alexandria, and it is believed that he brought the manuscript with him thence, when he was translated in 1621 to Constantinople. It is a beautiful book, written on pages of fine vellum measuring about $12\frac{1}{2}$ by $10\frac{1}{2}$ inches, with two columns of writing on each page. At present, bound in four volumes bearing the royal arms and initials of Charles I, it may be seen

56

any day in the British Museum, to which it passed with the rest of the Royal Library by the gift of George II in 1757. It contains the whole Greek Bible, complete except for accidental mutilations, which have caused the loss of nearly the whole of St. Matthew and substantial parts of the Psalms, St. John, and 2 Corinthians, and a few smaller mutilations elsewhere. In addition, it contains the third and fourth books of the Maccabees at the end of the Old Testament, and the two Epistles of Clement at the end of the New, while a table of contents shows that originally it had, at the end of all, the apocryphal Psalms of Solomon; but these, together with the end of 2 Clement, are now lost. In all, 773 leaves remain out of an original total of about 820.

The arrival of a manuscript of such antiquity made an instant sensation among scholars. Patrick Young, Librarian of the Royal Library, lost no time in publishing (in 1633) the Epistles of Clement, hitherto unknown, and made preparations for a complete edition of the whole. These came to nothing, but a collation of the principal readings in the New Testament was included in Bishop Walton's great Polyglot Bible in 1657. The Old Testament was eventually published in full in 1707-20, the New not until 1786; but its readings had been frequently collated and quoted before that. In modern times photographic facsimiles have been published by the British Museum, which for most purposes serve all the needs of scholars.

It was this discovery and its publication that set on foot the search for manuscripts, especially of the New Testament, and the tabulation of the variations of reading found in them. A period of search through the libraries of Europe now set in, resulting in a series of publications ranging over the next two centuries (and still continuing, as occasions serve, to-day) in which English and German scholars took the leading part. The "received" Greek text continued to be printed without alteration, but readings from various manuscripts were appended to it, and the manuscripts themselves were tabulated and numbered for easy reference. Uncial manuscripts were indicated by the capital letters of the Latin and Greek alphabets, minuscule manuscripts by arabic numerals; and this system has continued in force (with some necessary modifications) to the present day.

A few of the principal landmarks of this work may be noted. The sixteenth and seventeenth centuries saw the issue of a series of sumptuous editions of the Bible in several languages, hence known as the Polyglot Bibles. The first of these was the

Complutensian Polyglot (1522), already referred to,
which in six volumes contained the Old Testament
in Hebrew, Latin, and Greek (with interlinear
Latin translation), and the New Testament in Greek
and Latin. Next came the Antwerp Polyglot
(1569-72), in eight volumes, in which the Syriac
version was added (with a Latin translation); then
the Paris Polyglot (1629-45), in ten huge volumes,
which added Arabic (again with a Latin translation) and the Samaritan Pentateuch to the other
languages; and finally the London Polyglot (1657),
in eight volumes, edited by Brian Walton, in which
the total of languages reaches seven, viz. Hebrew
(Old Testament only), Greek, Latin, Syriac,
Ethiopic, Arabic and Persian (New Testament
only), with Latin translations attached in all cases,
besides the Samaritan Pentateuch and various
Targums or paraphrases. These massive volumes
may be found to-day on the shelves of the great
libraries, or in the ancient collections of colleges
and schools, and inspire one with awe at the
amount of labour involved in their compilation;
but none of them is of any critical value except the
last, in which Walton added in notes the readings of
the Codex Alexandrinus, and so made them available for the use of scholars. He also gave the readings of fifteen manuscripts, besides the fifteen used

59

by Stephanus, and among these authorities were
two of great age and value, the Codex Bezæ of the
Gospels and Acts (fifth century), and the Codex
Claromontanus of the Pauline Epistles (sixth
century).

The next steps forward were again made in
England. In 1675 Dr. John Fell, Dean of Christ
Church and hero of a celebrated stanza, printed a
critical apparatus in which he claims to have used
over a hundred manuscripts, adding a number from
the Bodleian to those which he derived from
Stephanus, Walton, and others, and using the
Coptic and Gothic versions. But the climax of
English work in the seventeenth century was that of
John Mill, who, encouraged and pecuniarily
assisted by Fell, laboured at the task of collecting
collations over more than a quarter of a century,
and eventually produced in 1707 a New Testament
in which he attached to the text of Stephanus the
various readings of seventy-eight other manuscripts
besides those used by Stephanus himself, with all
the versions to which he could get access, and (for
the first time) the quotations from the Scriptures of
the early Christian writers, the evidence of whom as
to the texts known to them is often of great value.
To all this he prefixed an elaborate introduction,
which may fairly be said to have laid the founda-

tions of the textual criticism of the New Testament. It was a great work, and, though assailed by some who thought that doubt was thrown on the integrity of the Scriptures by the presentation of so many various readings, remained as the basis for scholarly work on the New Testament for a long time to come. It was warmly defended by the great scholar, Richard Bentley, against those who foolishly thought that reverence for the Bible was better shown by accepting a faulty text without question than by facing the facts and endeavouring to arrive at the truth by a scholarly study of the evidence.

But for this hostile atmosphere, England might have anticipated by a century the work in which Germany eventually led the way, by applying the evidence thus collected to the revision of the text itself. Bentley himself (who certainly would have been deterred by no criticism) contemplated the preparation of an edition of the New Testament with a revised text, but never got beyond the collection of materials; but two scholars of less note, Edward Wells (in 1709–19) and William Mace, a Presbyterian minister (in 1729), produced such editions, on the basis of the evidence collected by Mill. Both editions were vehemently attacked in their own country, and they made no impression on the course of criticism; but modern German scholars have paid honourable tribute to them, pointing out that in a large majority of cases the corrections made by them in the received text have been confirmed by the scholarship of the nineteenth century. In their own country, however, they were prophets without honour, and little is heard of English contributions to the subject for the next century. On the Continent also text-revision was not in favour; but the work of collecting evidence and cataloguing manuscripts continued actively.

A Swiss pupil of Bentley's, J. J. Wetstein, was the first to compile a list of manuscripts with the method of nomenclature (as described above) which has since been generally followed. His list (published in 1751–2) comprised 21 uncial manuscripts, and over 250 minuscules. C. F. Matthaei added 57 manuscripts to the list in 1782–8, and a few more in 1803–7. Further additions by Alter from manuscripts in the Imperial Library at Vienna, and by three Danish professors from various libraries in Italy, Germany, and Spain, carried on the work to the end of the century; and in the early years of the nineteenth century all that hitherto had been done in the way of listing manuscripts was summed up and greatly extended by J. M. A. Scholz, who in 1830–6 published a catalogue of

62

New Testament manuscripts which included 26 uncials and 469 minuscules of the Gospels, 8 uncials and 192 minuscules of the Acts and Catholic Epistles, 9 uncials and 246 minuscules of the Pauline Epistles, and 3 uncials and 88 minuscules of the Apocalypse, besides 239 lectionaries, or collections of lessons for reading in church. Scholz's object was not to collate manuscripts, but to catalogue them, so that others might know what materials were in existence for them to work on; and his list, for all its defects, provided the basis on which the list has since been kept up, until now the total runs into the neighbourhood of five thousand.

The period during which the mere collection of material predominated over all other considerations may be said to extend from 1627, when the Codex Alexandrinus came to England, to 1830 when Scholz began to publish his catalogue—a period of two hundred years. A new period starts, as we shall see, in 1831; but meanwhile it may be useful to sum up what had been achieved. Exactness of figures is illusory, since some manuscripts contain the whole of the New Testament, while others (the large majority) contain only one section of it—the Gospels, or the Acts and Catholic Epistles, or the Pauline Epistles, or the Apocalypse; but it is within the limit to say that something over a thousand manuscripts had been brought to the knowledge of scholars. By far the greater part of these were minuscules—that is were of the tenth century or later; but among the uncials, which were of early date, were some of prime importance. The oldest and best of all, the Codex Vaticanus, was indeed known, since it had been in the Vatican Library since at least 1481; but though it had been used for Pope Sixtus' edition of the Septuagint, it had been little noticed in connection with the New Testament. Bentley had a collation made of it, but did not use it; other scholars examined it more or less casually; but it was not until after it had been brought to Paris by Napoleon, with other loot from Italy, that a German scholar, Hug, realized and proclaimed its age and value. When it was returned to Rome, after the fall of Napoleon, the Vatican authorities withheld it from foreign scholars, because they contemplated publishing it themselves; but their edition hung fire until 1857, and then was so badly executed as to be quite unserviceable. At the period at which we have arrived, therefore, it was for practical purposes still unknown, or at least unappreciated.

The only two manuscripts of the Gospels of the first rank that were fully known were the Codex Alexandrinus and the Codex Bezæ, both in England. The Alexandrinus had been collated by Walton and Mill and other editors, and was published in full in 1786; and its pre-eminence among New Testament manuscripts was generally recognized. The Codex Bezæ had been slightly used by Stephanus and Beza, and more fully collated by Walton and others, and was published in full in 1793 by the University of Cambridge; but its peculiar character, and its very marked divergences from the generally accepted text (as to which more will have to be said later) caused it to be regarded with suspicion, so that not much weight was attached to it. There were also two good and early manuscripts of other parts of the New Testament, the Codex Laudianus of the Acts at Oxford (published in full by Hearne in 1715) and the Codex Claromontanus of the Pauline Epistles at Paris, both of about the sixth century. It will be seen therefore that the scholars of this period had not much acquaintance with manuscripts of a really early date, and may be excused for having failed to realize the imperfections of the text to which they were accustomed. With a few exceptions, they were overwhelmed by the mass of later manuscripts, nearly all of which contained the relatively late Byzantine text which had entrenched itself in the " received text " of Stephanus.

There were some, however, who saw deeper and took the first steps towards testing the evidence by the application of scientific scholarship. Bentley would have done so, if his edition had ever come to the birth; but a few others actually achieved something, and their work, though it found little acceptance among their contemporaries, is held in honour to-day. Three scholars deserve particular mention, as having laid the foundations of the theory of the textual criticism of the New Testament on which we build to-day. The first is J. A. Bengel, who in an edition published in 1734 was the first to endeavour to classify the total mass of authorities and to distinguish the character and relative importance of different groups—in short, to consider the quality of the witnesses, and not only their quantity. He divided the witnesses (including versions as well as Greek manuscripts) into two groups, which he named African and Asian, the former including the few most ancient authorities, which appeared to emanate from Egypt and North Africa, and the latter the great mass of later manuscripts, containing what we have called the Byzantine or received text. J. S. Semler (1767) expanded this division into a threefold classification, *(a)* Alexandrian, which he attributed to Origen, and to which he assigned the earliest Greek manuscripts and the Syriac, Coptic, and Ethiopic versions, *(b)* Eastern, with its centres at Antioch and Constantinople, and including the main mass of authorities, and *(c)* Western, to be found in the Latin versions and Fathers. This thesis was elaborated and extended by his pupil, J. J. Griesbach, the greatest Biblical scholar of the eighteenth century, who in three editions published between 1774 and 1805 applied Semler's classification to the increased material collected by Wetstein, and allotted the several manuscripts, versions and Fathers precisely to the several groups. In the Alexandrian group he placed three uncials (including the early but incomplete Codex Ephraemi at Paris), six selected minuscules, the Coptic, Ethiopic, Armenian, and later Syriac (known as Harklean) versions, and the quotations in Origen, Clement of Alexandria, and Eusebius; in the Western, Codex Bezæ, the Latin versions, and sometimes the Peshitta Syriac; and in the Eastern or Constantinopolitan, the Codex Alexandrinus and the mass of later authorities. Like Bengel and Semler he regarded the small groups of early witnesses as altogether superior in weight to the numerically preponderant mass of the Constantinopolitan or Byzantine group.

This classification, though minuter criticism has modified it in some of its details, remains substanti-

67

ally the basis of modern textual theory. It rests first on the discernment that certain groups of authorities are linked together by internal agreements which show that they go back to some common ancestor or group of ancestors; secondly, that quality is to be preferred to quantity; thirdly, that quality can be discerned on grounds of internal probability. On the basis of these principles the conclusion is arrived at that the great mass of authorities represent a relatively late revision of the text, and that to find the truth we must look mainly to the small groups of witnesses which are either anterior to this revision or have partially escaped its influence. It was a doctrine wholly inacceptable to the age in which it was produced, and has been hotly disputed since, as we shall see; but it is the doctrine which has been universally applied by the editors of ancient classical texts, and is now accepted by practically all Biblical scholars. We shall reach the last stages in the controversy when we come to the English Revised Version of 1881.

CHAPTER VII

THE REVISION OF THE TEXT

WE have now arrived at a point, just over a hundred years ago, when a fresh start was made in Biblical criticism, and a period opens which is full of exciting incidents, lively controversy, and remarkable discoveries. By 1830, as we have seen, a stage had been reached when, through the labours of Scholz and his predecessors, a large mass of evidence had been catalogued and arranged for the use of scholars. A few efforts had been made, notably by Griesbach, to formulate principles for the scientific use of this evidence; but these had met with little acceptance from their contemporaries. The time had come when, under the impulse of the more critical spirit of the mid-nineteenth century, a fresh start could be made with a better chance of success, and a movement could be initiated which has gone on with ever-increasing momentum to our own day.

The prime mover in this was a German scholar, Carl Lachmann. He had been trained as a classical scholar and had edited classical texts, and it appeared to him that the problem of sifting out the true text of the New Testament from the divergent manuscripts in which it had been handed down to us was exactly the same as that which confronts an editor of Thucydides or Plato, and should be attacked in the same manner. The earliest manuscripts were likely to have suffered least from the accumulated errors of scribes or the revision of editors; therefore it was to them that we should look first, though keeping a vigilant eye on the possibility of errors in them also. The mass of late manuscripts could for most purposes be ignored. The " received text " of Stephanus was set aside, and the text was constructed *de novo* from the earliest authorities accessible to him. These included the codices Alexandrinus, Vaticanus (very imperfectly collated as yet), Ephraemi, Bezæ, Claromontanus, Laudianus, and a few uncial fragments, the two oldest manuscripts of the Latin Vulgate, and the writings of four or five of the earliest Fathers. The Syriac and Coptic versions were not used, because he did not know these languages. To eliminate the " personal equation," he followed in every case the majority of his selected authorities; and in this way he hoped to arrive, if not at the authentic original text, at least at the text as it was known about the time of the acceptance of Christianity by the Empire.

He began by printing a small edition of the New Testament in 1831, containing his revised text with very little explanation of the grounds on which he had arrived at it; and this was followed up in 1842–50 by a larger edition, containing fuller evidence and an exposition of his principles of criticism. His work was by no means perfect, and the materials at his disposal were much less than we have to-day; but by his outspoken rejection of the " received " text of 1550, and his bold application of textual science to the problems of the Bible, he did invaluable service, and lighted a fire which is still burning.

So far the search for manuscripts had been of a commonplace kind—merely the listing, and sometimes the collation, of volumes standing on the shelves of the principal libraries in Europe. Now a young man comes on the scene, who was to carry the search into more out-of-the-way places—the bindings of books, collections of miscellaneous sheets of old vellum, and libraries in more remote countries—who was to make a greater number of important additions to the list than any other scholar before or since, and who was to crown his career by the most sensational discovery in the history of scholarship, and by making known the two most valuable copies of the Bible in existence. This was Constantine Tischendorf (1815–74), who immediately after taking his degree in Theology at Leipzig in 1840 set out on his self-imposed task of searching out and publishing every fragment of an uncial manuscript of either Testament that he could find, together with not a few minuscules. The list of his discoveries is amazing. He discovered for the first time eighteen uncial manuscripts (all except five being mere fragments) and six minuscules; he was the first editor of twenty-five uncials (all fragments); he edited afresh eleven others, some (such as the Vaticanus, Ephraemi, Claromontanus and Laudianus) of the first importance; he transcribed four more, and collated thirteen. With the exception of the Alexandrinus and Codex Bezæ, there was no uncial manuscript of real importance to the knowledge of which Tischendorf did not contribute in greater or less degree.

Meanwhile he was producing edition after edition in which the results of his discoveries were incorporated. In all he produced eight editions of the Greek New Testament, four of the Latin, and four of the Septuagint, besides texts of the apocryphal gospels and epistles, and besides his editions of individual manuscripts. Following Lachmann, he cut himself free from the "received text," and depended mainly on the more ancient manuscripts; but his own reconstructed text fluctuated much according to his most recent studies and discoveries, so that his contribution to text-reconstruction is less important than his additions to the materials of criticism. Nevertheless his final edition of the Greek New Testament (1869–72), with its full textual apparatus, has remained the standard edition for the use of scholars, and is only now in process of being superseded by a new edition prepared in England on the same lines, but embodying the results of all those recent discoveries which Tischendorf did not live to see.

But the crowning achievements of his life were the discovery of the Codex Sinaiticus and the editing of the Codex Vaticanus. The story of the former has been much before the public lately on the occasion of the surprising acquisition of the manuscript by the British Museum from the Government of Soviet Russia; but so many myths were embroidered on it, and so many credulous people were led to believe them, that it may be well to tell it again. In soberest fact, it is a sufficiently romantic story. It was as a young man of 29, with three editions of the New Testament already to his credit, that Tischendorf set out to carry his researches further afield under the patronage of King Frederick Augustus of Saxony. In the course of this journey he visited the monastery of St. Catherine at Mount Sinai, and there, according to his story (which has successfully resisted all the criticism of those who have tried to discredit him), he one day saw in a basket a number of leaves of vellum with fine and obviously very early uncial writing on them, which he was informed were about to be destroyed, as many similar leaves had already been. He asked for and was allowed to keep these leaves, forty-three in number, which proved to contain portions of the Septuagint, from the books of 1 Chronicles, Jeremiah, Nehemiah, and Esther, written in a hand which struck him as looking older than anything he had ever seen. He also saw, but was not allowed to take away, a considerable number of leaves from the books of Isaiah and Maccabees. There was nothing to suggest that the manuscript included, or had ever included, the New Testament. Still, forty-three leaves of a Septuagint, perhaps as much as a century older than the celebrated Codex Alexandrinus, were no small haul, and Tischendorf returned in triumph to Leipzig, deposited his treasure in the University Library with the name of Frederick Augustus attached to it, edited it, but was careful not to say whence he had obtained it. He knew that there was more of it to

74

be had, and did not want to put anyone else on the track, so he merely said that the leaves appeared to have been always lying *perdus* in Egypt or at any rate in the neighbourhood of Egypt, which was true, but a very ingenious (and quite proper) economy of the truth. It was nine years later that he was able to revisit Sinai, but he could then obtain no news of the manuscript, and supposed that some more fortunate traveller had carried it off, perhaps an English officer of whose presence he heard rumours. Six years later he was back again, working at the manuscripts visible in the library of the monastery; but still no word of the lost treasure until, on the last evening of his stay, he chanced to show the steward of the monastery a copy of the edition of the Septuagint which he had produced a few years before. Whereupon the steward remarked that he also had a copy of the Septuagint, and taking from a shelf a parcel wrapped in a cloth he revealed to Tischendorf's astonished eyes a mass of leaves which he easily recognized as belonging to his long-coveted manuscript. It was a far greater prize than he had any reason to expect; for not only were there 199 more leaves of the Old Testament, but the whole New Testament, complete from beginning to end, with the Epistle of Barnabas and part of the " Shepherd " of Hermas. Tischendorf, beside him-

75

self with delight, sat up all night copying the Epistle
of Barnabas, and asked if he might take the manuscript to Cairo to copy. The Superior was absent,
and one monk objected, so Tischendorf departed
without it; but on applying to the Superior at
Cairo, where a branch of the monastery was established, the latter agreed, and sent a camel-rider to
fetch it, and at Cairo sheet by sheet was handed out
for him and his assistants to copy. Meanwhile
Tischendorf had suggested that the monks should
present the manuscript to the Tsar, as the protector
of the Greek Church; and as they desired the
Tsar's influence in connection with a disputed
election to the Archbishopric of Sinai, they were
inclined to accept the proposal. The negotiations
dragged on a long time, as they are apt to do in the
East; but after nine months Tischendorf was
allowed to take the Codex to St. Petersburg, in
order to superintend the printing of it, and shortly
afterwards the desired appointment of the Archbishop was made. Throughout Tischendorf acted
in full accord with the heads of the monastery, and
when the Tsar delayed to make the return gift which
Eastern practice expected, he again intervened, and
procured the gift of the very substantial sum (for
those days) of 9,000 roubles and a number of
coveted decorations.

The correctness of Tischendorf's action throughout is established beyond question by the contemporary records, which make it clear that the monks parted with the manuscript (which they had so little valued in the past) willingly and for value received. It is only subsequent generations that have regretted that they did not open their mouths wider. The generation that made the " gift " was satisfied, and Tischendorf remained on good terms with them to the end of his life.

That Tischendorf also was satisfied goes without saying. He had brought to light a manuscript of the whole of the New Testament and nearly half the Old, a hundred years older than any extant manuscript except the very imperfectly known Vaticanus. It is a magnificent book, written with four columns to the page of the most beautiful uncial writing on pages of fine vellum measuring 15 by 13½ inches, and in admirable preservation. It was published in full by Tischendorf in facsimile type in 1862, some sheets of it being shown at the Great Exhibition in London in that year; and in 1911 the Oxford University Press published a photographic facsimile of the New Testament, followed by the Old Testament in 1922, both from photographs taken by Professor Kirsopp Lake and under his editorship. At St. Petersburg it remained for nearly three-quarters of a century, until the Soviet Government resolved to sell it, and after somewhat protracted negotiations it entered the British Museum at Christmas, 1933, there, it may be hoped, to find its lasting home, side by side with the Alexandrinus.

A comic episode attended the romance of its discovery, which was revived at the time of its purchase by the Museum. An ingenious Greek, by name Simonides, had about 1855 brought to England some manuscripts, among which was one which purported to be a history of Egypt by a Greek author named Uranius. This imposed even upon some of the elect, and an eminent German scholar, Dindorf, prepared an edition of it for the Oxford Press. Some sheets of it were already printed off when another German scholar observed that the chronology was unmistakably copied from a modern work. The forgery was obvious, and the work was hurriedly suppressed; such sheets of it as have survived are a rare bibliographical curiosity. (Subsequently, it may be added, Simonides purported to find among the Egyptian collections of a Liverpool gentleman a papyrus manuscript of St. Matthew written fifteen years after the Ascension, and portions of first-century papyri of the Epistles of SS. James and Jude, with other surprising things,

78

which he published in the same year as the Sinaiticus, but which failed to carry conviction of their genuineness. They may still be seen in Liverpool to-day, and considering how little was then known about papyri they are very ingenious productions.) Now Tischendorf had been concerned in the Uranius controversy, and Simonides had a grudge against him. Accordingly he proclaimed that, while the Uranius was genuine, he *had* himself written the whole of the Sinaiticus, having copied it in about six months in 1840 at Mount Athos from a Moscow edition of the Greek Bible ! The story teems with impossibilities. In 1840 Simonides was only 15 years old. He could not have obtained 350 leaves of ancient vellum. He could not have copied it in the time claimed. The manuscript is not written by a single hand, but by at least three different scribes, and has corrections by several others. No Moscow Bible from which it could have been copied exists. The whole story is one of the comedies of crime, amusing but not deserving a moment's serious consideration.

Having thus published the Sinaiticus in 1862, Tischendorf turned his attention to the Vaticanus, of which two editions by Cardinal Mai had been published in 1857 and 1859, which differed so much from one another that both were evidently untrustworthy. Tischendorf visited Rome in 1866, and with difficulty obtained permission to examine particular passages of it over a period of fourteen days, with only three working hours in each day. He exceeded the terms of his permission, however, by copying twenty pages in full, and the manuscript was withdrawn. Nevertheless with the results of his examination he was able to publish in 1867 an edition which went far towards placing the evidence of this supremely important manuscript in the hands of scholars; and this was supplemented in 1868 by an edition of the New Testament (followed in later years by the Old Testament) prepared for the Vatican itself by Vercellone and Cozza.

In this manner New Testament scholars had in their hands by the end of 1868 two great copies of the sacred books earlier by a century than those they had hitherto been able to use. A powerful stimulus was thus given to the demand for a thorough revision of the Greek text in common use; for these two great manuscripts plainly did not support the " received " text, and in the eyes of nearly all trained scholars were evidently superior to it. Tischendorf himself issued in 1869–72 a revised text of the New Testament based predominantly on the Vaticanus and Sinaiticus, and provided with a full apparatus of various readings from all the important extant texts and the principal versions and quotations in the early Fathers. This edition remains to-day the most serviceable critical edition for the use of scholars, though much needing to be brought up to date by incorporating the results of the later discoveries which we have still to describe —a task which has lately been taken up by an English committee, and of which the first part (the Gospel of St. Mark, edited by the Rev. S. C. E. Legg) was published early in 1935.

In England especially the need for revision was strongly felt, and the response to it took two forms. On the one hand, two great Cambridge scholars, Westcott and Hort, undertook the preparation of a revised Greek text of the New Testament, with a full statement of the principles on which it was based; on the other hand, a committee was appointed by the Convocation of Canterbury in 1870 to prepare a revised edition of the English Bible. Both undertakings went on side by side, and the results of both, so far as the New Testament was concerned, were given to the world simultaneously in May, 1881. Westcott and Hort were members of the Revision Committee, and carried very great weight with it; so that the Revised Version, though not wholly representing their views, is so largely coloured by them, and their edition of the

81

Greek text has had such an epoch-making influence on all subsequent textual criticism, that some account of their theories is essential for the understanding of the problems with which we have to deal to-day. Westcott and Hort made the fullest use of the materials with which Tischendorf had provided them; indeed, the outstanding characteristic of their work is the predominant importance which they attach to the Vaticanus, to which the Sinaiticus takes second place. Working on the lines already laid down by Griesbach, as described above, they divided all the authorities into four groups or families: (1) a group which they called *Neutral,* headed by the Vaticanus and Sinaiticus, but supported more or less by some eight or ten imperfect and later uncial manuscripts, by a handful of minuscules which have more or less escaped revision to the standard form, by the Coptic versions (of which the earlier, or Sahidic, was at this time very imperfectly known), and by the great Christian scholar of the early third century, Origen: (2) a small and rather ill-defined group of authorities, domiciled in Egypt, but not conforming to the Vaticanus-group, which they called *Alexandrian*: (3) a family which they called *Western,* because its principal representatives are the Old Latin version and the Codex Bezæ (which has a Latin text in

82

addition to the Greek), but of which traces are to be found in several minuscule manuscripts, in the only manuscript of the Old Syriac version then known, and, above all, in nearly all the quotations in the earliest Christian writers; a family important by its age, and remarkable for its very marked deviations (especially in Luke and Acts) both from the Neutral and from the "received" text: (4) the great mass of later authorities, which they denominated *Syrian*, because they thought that this type of text, which eventually dominated the whole Eastern Church, had its origin in a revision that began in the neighbourhood of Antioch in Syria about the end of the fourth century. The "Syrian" family they ruled out, as Griesbach and Lachmann had done, because (as they were the first to point out) not only were the authorities containing it relatively late, but no readings characteristic of it are to be found in any writer before Chrysostom, who worked in Antioch in the last years of the fourth century. The "Western" type they regarded as intrinsically inferior to the "Neutral," and as losing authority on account of the great differences between the various members of the group. The "Alexandrian" only differed from the Neutral in relatively unimportant details; but the "Neutral," and especially the Vaticanus, they believed to represent a tradition which had descended with no serious corruption from the earliest times. To the Neutral group, therefore, they pinned their faith almost exclusively, and departed from the Vaticanus only in a few special instances, or in cases of obvious scribal errors.

In Westcott and Hort, therefore, the Biblical student at last had a Greek text based on the most ancient authorities, and with a fully expounded textual theory to support it. And the English reader had in the Revised Version a translation which, though not taken directly or fully from Westcott and Hort's text, at least represented a text far sounder than the " received text " which had been in the hands of the makers of the Authorised Version, and had since been in universal use. So far, all was clear gain. Unfortunately, however, the Revisers had not obeyed the instruction which enjoined on them " to introduce as few alterations as possible into the text of the Authorised Version consistently with faithfulness," or at least they had given an exaggerated interpretation to " faithfulness." A multitude of small changes made in obedience to a somewhat pedantic scholarship, and not governed by the instinctive sense of style which was the heritage of King James's translators, repelled the reader who found the most familiar passages in the most familiar

84

part of his Bible (the Gospels) presented to him in a changed form for which he could see no good reason. The result has been fatal to the general acceptance of the Revised Version as a substitute for the Authorised; but this should not make us blind to its real merits. Where the difference between the two is due to a difference in the text translated, it is long odds that the Revised Version is right; though more recent scholarship would in some cases prefer the alternative readings which (from excessive caution in the acceptance of variants) have been relegated to the marginal notes. Also in the Epistles many a difficult passage has been made more clear as the result of centuries of study of St. Paul's meaning. It is in the Gospels that the changes have been most unfortunate; and as the Gospels are the books best known to the majority of readers, this has prejudiced the whole. The Revised Version of the Old Testament, moreover, which followed in 1885, is not open to the same criticisms. Here the Revisers had not to deal with a new text, for the Hebrew text before them was substantially the same as in 1611, and they did not undertake to introduce changes from the Septuagint. On the other hand, the understanding of Hebrew had made much advance since the Authorised Version, and the Revisers were able to give

85

light to many an obscure passage, especially in the Prophets. In general, they were chary of making alterations unless the sense demanded it, and in most cases they were dealing with words less familiar than the Gospels. Consequently their work gave less offence, and the gain was generally recognized.

No serious student of the Bible in English can neglect the Revised Version without loss. While it never can be the magnificent monument of English which the Authorised Version is, while it cannot bring the sacred story and teaching home to us with the same unequalled appeal of majestic language, it does give us a more accurate text, translated with a more fully informed scholarship; and if we want to be sure of the meaning of the Bible we must always keep an eye on the Revised Version. Every educated student of the Bible should have and use both—the one for the edification which comes from great literature greatly expressed, the other for the more exact study of the true meaning of the Word of Life.

CHAPTER VIII

THE AGE OF DISCOVERIES

THE publication of the Revised New Testament by the two University Presses on May 17, 1881, was the most sensational event in the annals of publishing. The public curiosity was intense, and the demand for early copies overwhelming. Bribes of as much as £5,000 had been offered for advance copies in vain. The Oxford Press alone sold a million copies on the first day. All day the streets about Paternoster Row were blocked by a stream of wagons carrying them to the railways for distribution. Five days later two Chicago newspapers printed the entire book as a supplement to their ordinary issue, half of the text having been received by telegraph before actual copies were available. A period of lively controversy followed, the new version being bitterly attacked by a few scholars (headed by Dean Burgon) who refused to abandon the " received " text, maintaining that the authority of the Church outweighed the evidence of ancient

87

manuscripts and the ordinary canons of textual scholarship. These critics had behind them the general unwillingness of the public to accept changes in words so well known and so much loved as those of the Bible; and for some time the Revision had a ſtormy passage. The verdict of scholars was overwhelmingly in favour of the revised Greek text as againſt the old "received" text, and this issue may be taken as decided; but time has rather increased than diminished the weight of criticism of the literary shortcomings of the English. Increased knowledge (due in part to the discoveries of Greek papyri in Egypt) of the Greek in common use in the firſt century has shown that many of the verbal changes introduced by the Revisers were due to a pedantic application of the principles of classical Greek to a popular language which ignored them. And so opinion settled down to the general conclusions described in the laſt chapter.

It might have looked, and indeed did look, in 1881 as though the end of a period had been reached. Scholars had a new Greek text, based upon the moſt ancient aⅰthorities in accordance with the beſt principles of textual scholarship; and English readers had a revised English Bible based upon this Greek text. It looked as if nothing now remained to be done but to digeſt these results, and

88

that further changes were not to be expected. Yet, as a matter of fact, a new period was just opening which may rightly be called the Age of Discoveries, since the half-century which has followed since 1881 has seen discovery after discovery widening our knowledge of the Bible text and its early history, and testing the results at which the scholars of 1881 had arrived by evidence with which they were totally unacquainted. It is the story of these discoveries which has now to be told—discoveries which have gone on up to the time of writing, and to which more additions may be made before these pages are finished; and then an attempt will be made to sum up the results.

The discovery of the Codex Sinaiticus in the monastery of St. Catherine at Mount Sinai was the climax of the previous period, and it was from the same spot that the first discoveries of the new period came. First, in 1889, Dr. Rendel Harris found there a Syriac translation of a lost Christian work, the *Apology* of Aristides, a defence of Christianity addressed to the emperor Antoninus Pius by an Athenian philosopher about A.D. 140, very valuable for the early history and creed of the Christian community. A very curious result followed; for it appeared that the *Apology* had never really been lost at all, but that the original Greek had been embedded in a Christian romance composed about the seventh century, though hitherto there had been no means of identifying it, nor any reason to suppose that it was any earlier than the work in which it had been incorporated. Thus one more early Christian work was restored to our knowledge.

The next discovery was more distinctly Biblical. Encouraged by Dr. Rendel Harris's success, two Cambridge ladies, Mrs. Lewis and Mrs. Gibson, twin sisters and highly accomplished Orientalists, made another visit to Mount Sinai to search for treasures. Among other manuscripts which they examined, one was a palimpsest; that is, the original writing had been partly washed out, and another text written over it. The lower writing was seen to be a copy of the Gospels in Syriac, which might easily be important because of its evidently early date; so they took photographs of it and brought them home for detailed examination. Then it appeared that they had discovered a real prize; for it turned out to be, not the ordinary Syriac version of the Gospels (known as the Peshitta), but an earlier version, of which only one copy was hitherto known, and that very imperfect. This was a manuscript acquired by the British Museum in 1842, printed and privately circulated by Cureton in 1848, and finally published in

1858. It contained portions of the Gospels of Matthew, Luke and John, but of Mark only the laſt four verses. The new Sinaitic manuscript had portions of all Gospels, and evidently represented the same version as the Curetonian manuscript, but with considerable variations. Thus, while the Curetonian must originally have contained the disputed ending of Mark (xvi. 9–20), the Sinaitic did not, ending the Gospel with verse 8, as do the Vaticanus and Sinaiticus and the earlieſt manuscript of the Old Latin version. On the whole, the Sinaitic Syriac appeared to represent the version in a rather earlier form than the Curetonian, besides supplementing many of its lacunæ; so that we now had a subſtantial knowledge of this earlieſt Syriac translation.

Now this was a discovery of firſt-class importance; for this Syriac version is one of the earlieſt translations of the New Teſtament, having probably been made before the end of the second century, and we now had two witnesses for it, both written in the fifth century or earlier. The translation muſt have been made from Greek manuscripts in exiſtence in the second century, which thus carries us back to a period long before our earlieſt Greek manuscripts. Further, it was apparent that this Old Syriac text differed in many details from the type represented by the Vaticanus

91

and Sinaiticus, to which Westcott and Hort had given the name of " Neutral," and which they maintained to be the best. It differed from it in very much the same way (though not always in the same passages) as did the Latin group which Westcott and Hort called " Western." While, therefore, in many passages it reinforced the Neutral text as against the " received " or Byzantine text, it also gave strong support to those who were disposed to question Westcott and Hort's exclusive trust in the Neutral.

This was the more important, because by this time the centre of controversy with regard to the Bible text had shifted. At first, as has already been described, it was a contest between the adherents of the Byzantine text, which had so long dominated the Christian world, and the earlier types represented by a comparatively small number of authorities. That contest had been quickly decided, in the eyes of scholars, in favour of the earlier types, and the Byzantine text had been accepted as secondary and of relatively late origin. But the argument which ruled out the Byzantine text, viz. that readings characteristic of it were not found in Christian writers before the latter part of the fourth century, could not be used against the type of text which Westcott and Hort had labelled

"Western." On the contrary, it was evident that all the early Christian writers, with the partial exception of Origen, had used texts which did not conform with the "Neutral" type. If, therefore, all early non-Neutral readings could be grouped together in a single family, as the Neutral authorities were, there was good ground for claiming that this, rather than the Neutral family, had the support of the earliest patristic evidence. Many prominent scholars were inclined to take this view; and the issue now lay, not between "Neutral" and "Byzantine," but between "Neutral" and "Western." Consequently the old Syriac version, which was certainly pre-Byzantine and non-Neutral, was hailed as an ally by the Westerners, and the position of Westcott and Hort, with their almost exclusive dependence on the Vaticanus, was to that extent shaken. As will be seen later, there were considerable qualifications to be made to this argument, but for the moment this was the general impression.

The question of the early Syriac text of the Gospels was complicated by another consideration to which attention must be drawn, both because of its own importance and because of a curious series of discoveries (one very recent) connected with it. It was known from early Christian writers that an Assyrian Christian named Tatian, who was born about A.D. 120, had produced about A.D. 170 a work called *Diatessaron* (" Concordance of Four "), which was generally supposed to be a harmony of the four Gospels. The work, however, seemed to be completely lost, and the followers of the German school who about the middle of the nineteenth century maintained that none of our Gospels was written before about A.D. 140, and that therefore they are of little historical authority, denied that it was a concordance of our Gospels at all. So late as 1876 the anonymous author of an able work called *Supernatural Religion* strenuously maintained this point of view, even going so far as to deny that the work had ever existed; and Bishop Lightfoot, who used his immense learning to defend the authenticity and early date of the Gospels, could only bring arguments from probability against him. Yet all the time the decisive proof was lying, so to speak, under their noses. So far back as 1836 the Fathers of a convent in Venice had printed an Armenian version of a commentary by St. Ephrem (who lived in the fourth century) on this very work, which proved beyond doubt that it was in fact a concordance of the four canonical Gospels. Since, however, Armenian was a language almost unknown to Western scholars, no one took any notice of it; but in 1876, just before the appearance of

Supernatural Religion, a Latin translation of this commentary was published by the same Fathers, which ought to have brought it to the notice of Biblical students. Strange to say, neither of the learned controversialists was aware of its existence, and it was not until 1880 that Dr. Ezra Abbot called attention to it. This at once led to further research, and first one and then another copy was discovered of an Arabic translation of the *Diatessaron* itself, which was published in 1888.

These discoveries finally disposed of any doubt as to what the *Diatessaron* was, and proved that by about A.D. 170 the four canonical Gospels held an undisputed pre-eminence over all other narratives of our Saviour's life; but they left several questions undetermined. Being in Arabic, it was not always certain what the exact text was from which it was translated; and scholars differed as to the original language of the *Diatessaron*. Was it originally composed in Greek or in Syriac? Since it unquestionably circulated mainly in the Syriac Church (though it was certainly also translated into Latin), and since the Arabic version was certainly made from the Syriac, many scholars were led to suppose that Syriac was its original language. Others, however, pointing to the fact that its title is Greek, maintained that it was first composed in Greek and then translated, in Tatian's own lifetime, into Syriac. In any case it is probably at least as old as the Old Syriac Gospels represented by the Sinaitic and Curetonian manuscripts, and it was in this form that the Gospels mainly circulated in the early Church in Syria. What its exact text was, and what influence it exerted on the text of the separate Gospels, remains uncertain, for the Arabic translation (which was probably made about A.D. 900) has unquestionably been partly assimilated, as almost invariably happens, to later texts; and it still remains one of the riddles which Bible students have to solve.

Here a most interesting, though rather tantalizing, discovery has to be recorded, which has only been made public within the last few years. Far away, on the banks of the Euphrates, the ruins of a Roman fort were discovered at a place called Dura by some English officers in 1920, just before the withdrawal of the British troops. What first attracted attention was some very remarkable wall-paintings of the first century and somewhat later. Subsequently (since the site fell into the French mandated area) it was systematically investigated by French and American excavators. It was discovered that in the last years of the Roman occupation of the fort (which was taken by the Persians in A.D. 256) the walls had been strengthened by the destruction of a quantity of houses, including a Christian church and a Jewish synagogue, and among the debris were found a number of papyri and vellum manuscripts which had been protected against damp in a manner to be paralleled only in Egypt. Among these, when they were examined at Yale in 1933, was found a vellum fragment of a copy of the *Diatessaron* in *Greek*. It is only a small scrap, consisting of some fourteen imperfect lines, containing the narrative of the petition of Joseph of Arimathæa for the body of our Lord, written in a hand of the first half of the third century (it must of course have been earlier than the destruction of A.D. 256). It is a mosaic made up of phrases from all four canonical Gospels, with some editorial adjustments. Small as it is, it throws some light on Tatian's method of compilation, showing that he dealt freely with his materials and did not give a general preference to any one evangelist. But its chief interest is that it shows that the *Diatessaron* circulated in Greek in a distant corner of Syria, about half a century after its composition. This has some bearing on the problem of its original language. If it had been composed in Syriac, it would naturally have circulated in Syria in that language, and the subsequent translations into Greek and

Latin would have been reserved for countries in which those languages predominated; whereas if it were originally composed in Greek, it might have had some circulation in that language, even in Syria, before a Syriac translation was available. The proof is not decisive, since a military and trading ſtation, such as Dura, would have had inhabitants who were not Syrians, and they might have brought a Greek copy of the work with them; but so far as it goes, it adds something to the case of those who advocate a Greek original, and in any case it proves that the *Diatessaron* exiſted in Greek before A.D. 250.

For the next discovery we muſt return from Meso-potamia to our familiar hunting-ground of Egypt. In the winter of 1906 an American gentleman, Mr. Charles L. Freer of Detroit, owner of a world-famous collection of Chinese and Japanese paint-ings which he has inſtalled in a museum in Wash-ington, was travelling in Egypt, and saw in the possession of a Cairo dealer a group of vellum manuscripts, or portions of manuscripts, of obvi-ously early character and Biblical in their contents. They did not come within the scope of his normal intereſts as a collector, but he realized the impor-tance of the opportunity and secured them. By so doing, he acquired for the United States one of the earlieſt copies of the Gospels in Greek that has come down to us.

The collection as a whole comprised four manuscripts, two of the Old Teſtament and two of the New. Firſt there was a volume containing the books of Deuteronomy and Joshua, written in the sixth, or possibly the late fifth century. The numbering of the leaves shows that it originally contained the earlier books of the Pentateuch, from Genesis to Numbers, as well; and it may have had Judges and Ruth at the end, to complete the Octateuch. The second was a very fragmentary and much-damaged copy of the Psalter, which when found was juſt a solid lump of vellum that had suffered much from worms and damp. The moſt delicate skill and patience were necessary for its reſtoration, and even so, every leaf is imperfect, and of the earlier Psalms very little has survived. From the character of the handwriting, it appears to be of the sixth or seventh century, while the final quire, which no doubt replaces one that had been damaged at an earlier date, is probably of the ninth.

Of the New Teſtament manuscripts, one was of the Gospels, while the other originally contained the Acts, Catholic Epiſtles and Pauline Epiſtles but the earlier portion, from Acts to Romans, has been wholly loſt, and the reſt is very imperfect

It is indeed only a collection of fragments, in as bad condition as the Psalter above described. In date it is not earlier than the sixth century, but it has a good type of text of the same character as the Sinaiticus, Alexandrinus and Vaticanus. The Gospels Codex is far more perfect and important. It contains all four Gospels, in an order which was not unusual in the West, viz. Matthew, John, Luke, Mark, which probably reflects the order of their popularity. Its writing is unlike those of the other early uncials, being a small, sloping hand which is rather difficult to date, but may be assigned to the fifth, or possibly the fourth century. The first quire of John is later, having been apparently inserted about the seventh century to replace one that was damaged or defective.

The text of this Washington Codex, as it is called, has some very curious features. It is by no means uniform in character, and must have been copied from several ancestors which did not belong to the same textual group. Thus (to use the classification of Westcott and Hort), Matthew is Syrian (i.e. Byzantine); Mark i–v. 30 is Western; the rest of Mark does not conform to any of these groups, but to one which will have to be mentioned later; Luke i–viii. 12 is Neutral; the rest of Luke is Syrian; John i–v. 12 (the added quire) is

Syrian; and the rest of John is Neutral. One must therefore conclude that this Codex was copied from a group of papyrus rolls which differed among themselves in textual character, and that the same exemplar was not even followed through a whole Gospel. This would only have been possible in a library where many copies of the Scriptures were available, and the scribe was not particular as to the text he was copying. This is quite natural when we remember that each book originally circulated in a separate roll, and there are other manuscripts which similarly have a different character in different parts (e.g. the Alexandrinus shows an early form of the Byzantine text in the Gospels, but elsewhere is Neutral); but one does not often see signs of so complicated a parentage as here.

One peculiar feature in the Washington Codex attracted immediate attention. It contains the disputed last twelve verses of Mark, but in the middle of them, after verse 14, is inserted the following additional passage:

And they answered and said, This generation of lawlessness and faithlessness is under Satan, who doth not allow the truth of God to prevail over the unclean things of the spirits. Therefore make manifest thy righteousness. So spake they now to Christ, and Christ said unto them, The tale of the years of the dominion of Satan is fulfilled, but other terrible things draw near, and by reason of the sins of them I was delivered over unto death, that they may return to the truth and sin no more; that they may inherit the spiritual and incorruptible glory of righteousness which is in heaven.

The first two sentences were known from a reference in one of the writings of St. Jerome, who says that they were found in some copies of the Gospel, chiefly Greek ones; but the rest was entirely new. No one would suppose the passage to be authentic, but it shows how additions were liable to be made in copies of the Gospels and to obtain some circulation.

The next stage of our textual history affords an interesting example of the results of intensive study completed by happy discovery. While the search for early manuscripts of the Bible was proceeding with the results already described, scholars had not neglected the study of the later manuscripts, on the chance of some of them having preserved traces of early types of text. So far back as 1877 two Irish scholars, W. H. Ferrar and T. K. Abbott, had published a study of four manuscripts which presented some peculiar features. Three of them were written in Southern Italy in the twelfth or thirteenth century; the fourth, now at Leicester, was written in England in the fifteenth century, but was evidently copied from a parent of the same family as the other three. The group is known as Family 13, from the number given in the lists to the first of them, or as the Ferrar Group, from the scholar who first called attention to them. They were plainly related, having peculiar readings which were not known elsewhere, or were only paralleled in very early manuscripts. A few other manuscripts were afterwards found to have traces of the same type; but it was not clear what significance or importance was to be attached to the peculiarities of a relatively late group, as to which all that could be said was that it seemed to have some affinity with the Old Syriac version. Its most outstanding variant was that it transferred the incident of the woman taken in adultery from St. John's Gospel (to which it certainly does not belong, being quite different in style and language) to a place in St. Luke, after xxi. 38.

Another little group of four manuscripts was similarly isolated by Professor Kirsopp Lake, who published an account of them in 1902. It is headed by the manuscript which stands first in the catalogue of minuscules (and was slightly used by Erasmus), and is therefore known as Family 1. It preserves many readings which are found in early manuscripts such as the Vaticanus and Sinaiticus and Codex Bezæ, or in the Old Syriac version, and Lake noticed that its peculiarities were most frequent

103

in St. Mark, where it also seemed to show some affinity with Family 13. Once attention had been called to this point, it was observed that in other manuscripts also St. Mark seemed to have been less affected than the other Gospels by the process of revision which produced the Byzantine text. The reason no doubt is that St. Mark, being the shortest Gospel, and containing less of the teaching of our Lord, was less often copied in early days and consequently less subject to alterations either by copyists or by editors. We have already seen that St. Mark displayed special characteristics in the Washington Codex, and we shall find the same in some other discoveries which have yet to be described.

The next step forward came from an unexpected quarter. In 1906, Professor von Soden, who was engaged in a very comprehensive edition of the Greek New Testament, called attention to a late and uncouth uncial manuscript (now at Tiflis) which had belonged to a monastery in the Caucasus called Koridethi. It did not seem to be earlier than the ninth century and its scribe evidently knew very little Greek; but perhaps for this very reason he was not likely to make alterations (though he might and did make many mistakes) in the text he was copying, and he had certainly preserved a somewhat unusual text. Von Soden associated it with Codex Bezæ, but in this he was certainly wrong; and when it was eventually published in full in 1913, it was pointed out by Lake and others that at any rate in Mark it had ftrong affinities with Families 1 and 13. The next ftage therefore was to combine this manuscript (to which the letter Θ (theta) was assigned in the catalogue of uncials) with those two families, and to designate the whole as Family Theta.

The significance of the little Ferrar group was thus evidently growing in importance, but it took on altogether a new aspect when in 1924 Canon Streeter published (in his book *The Four Gospels*) the results of his researches into it. After emphasizing the connection of this Family Θ with the Old Syriac version (which was a proof of its antiquity, in spite of the relatively late date of the manuscripts preserving it), he eftablished the remarkable faft that the great Christian scholar Origen (who died in A.D. 253) had in his later works, written after his removal from Egypt to Cæsarea in A.D. 231, used a text of this type. Cæsarea in Paleftine was a noted centre of Biblical ftudy, afterwards famous for a library of which the manuscripts used by Origen formed a conspicuous part, which was much used by St. Jerome, and in which there is good reason to believe the Codex Sinaiticus was at an early stage in its history. Streeter's conclusion therefore was that whereas Origen in his earlier works, written in Egypt, had used manuscripts containing the Alexandrian or Neutral type of text, he had found at Cæsarea a different type which he had accepted as superior and had thenceforth used, and which for us was represented by Family Θ. He accordingly gave this family a new name, as the " Cæsarean " text, to be equated with Hort's " Neutral " and " Western " as a family of first-rate importance.

This seemed to be a neat and compact, as well as important, result whereby the original insignificant Ferrar Group, of unknown origin, had been transformed into the Cæsarean text, backed by the authority of the greatest scholar of the early Church, and comfortably housed in Palestine, in appropriate proximity to the Church of Syria. It was, however, almost immediately disturbed; for Professor Lake showed that, on a closer analysis of the quotations in Origen's writings, it appeared that in his first works produced after his migration to Cæsarea he unquestionably used an Alexandrian text, and only later changed over to the Cæsarean. There is also some indication (though weak, for lack of sufficient evidence) that in his last work at

Alexandria he was using a Cæsarean text. While therefore it may be legitimate to label this text as Cæsarean, as having been used there by Origen and his disciple Eusebius, the truth may be that Origen brought it with him from Egypt, that he found manuscripts of the Alexandrian type at Cæsarea and for a time used them, but then reverted to the Cæsarean and thenceforth adhered to it.

Another useful point made by Streeter was that the Washington Gospels might be added to the growing list of Cæsarean authorities in respect of the greater part of St. Mark, the character of which, as indicated above, had hitherto been unidentified. The Georgian version has also been shown to be Cæsarean in character; and if, as is probable, the Georgian version was derived from the Syriac, this is further evidence for the connection of this type with Syria. From all these discussions and discoveries one certain fact emerges, that the Cæsarean text is now a definitely established entity, the character of which demands the further close study which it will undoubtedly receive from scholars.

CHAPTER IX

THE AGE OF DISCOVERIES (Continued): THE
CHESTER BEATTY PAPYRI

THE major discoveries of the period between 1881
and 1930 have now been mentioned, and they are
sufficient to give this half-century a special distinction in the history of the Bible. But they were
accompanied by a multitude of smaller ones, which
deserve a brief mention. Vellum manuscripts of
some importance continued to come to light; in
particular, four handsome volumes, of about the
sixth century, emerged from various out-of-the-way
places, one from Rossano, in Southern Italy, one
from Albania, one from Cappadocia, and one from
Sinope on the Black Sea. Two of them contained
illustrations, and must have been very sumptuous
volumes when complete. All are connected in
character, and represent an early stage in the production of the Byzantine text. Another uncial
manuscript of good character, especially in Mark,
was discovered by Gregory on Mount Athos; it is

interesting as having the shorter ending to Mark (in place of *vv.* 9–20), which is referred to in the marginal note in our Revised Version. Some hundreds of minuscule manuscripts were also added to the list, mainly from monasteries in the East; but these are mostly of small importance.

Meanwhile the flood of papyri from Egypt, which we have already mentioned as having begun in 1877 and still more significantly in 1890, was continuing unabated. One of these, though not strictly speaking Biblical, had a special interest for Christian students. This was a leaf, discovered by Grenfell and Hunt at Oxyrhynchus and published in 1897, containing several " Sayings of Jesus," or, as they are commonly called from the Greek word meaning "sayings" or "oracular utterances," " Logia." These, though they can have little claim to authenticity, and are akin to some sayings recorded in early Christian writings, are remarkable and even impressive in character. For instance: " Jesus saith, Wherever there are two, they are not without God, and wherever there is one alone, I say, I am with him. Raise the stone, and there thou shalt find me; cleave the wood, and there am I." Or again: " Jesus saith, Let not him who seeks cease until he finds, and when he finds he shall be astonished; astonished he shall reach the kingdom, and having reached the kingdom he shall reſt." In 1903 a second leaf, evidently from the same work, though not from the same manuscript, was discovered, and published in 1904. The second quotation above comes from this leaf.[1]

Of the Biblical papyri, which were not numerous, the only one of much size was one which contained a considerable part of the Epiſtle to the Hebrews, written on the back of an Epitome of Livy.[2] This (which is probably of the late fourth century) is of some importance in view of the fact that the Vaticanus lacks the latter part of this Epiſtle. The reſt were small fragments, individually of slight importance, but collectively of some value as showing that the Neutral type of text was by no means universally current in Egypt in the third and fourth centuries, to which moſt of them belong. Two of them (which have small portions of Acts) are rather definitely " Weſtern," and none of them are exclusively " Neutral," though several include readings of that type. None of the earlier fragments are Byzantine. Though their evidence with regard to particular readings does not amount

[1] The firſt leaf of the *Logia* is now in the Bodleian, the second in the British Museum.

[2] Originally published as Oxyrhynchus papyrus 657; now Brit. Mus. 1532.

to much, they are of value as throwing a little light on the general character of the type or types of text current in Egypt during this period. Papyri of the Old Testament are of more importance, including two of portions of the Minor Prophets (one in the Freer collection at Washington and one, a late codex, at Heidelberg), two of the Psalms (British Museum and Leipzig), and one of Genesis at Berlin.[1]

Papyri have also been of considerable importance in respect of the Sahidic or Old Coptic version. Of this a large number of fragments (sometimes containing Greek and Coptic texts in parallel columns) and a few substantial manuscripts have come to light. Some of these relate to the Old Testament, notably a complete Psalter of about the seventh century, now in the British Museum, and a less perfect one, on tiny leaves measuring about 3 inches by $2\frac{3}{4}$, in the Freer collection at Washington. But more important than these are a codex in the British Museum containing Deuteronomy, Jonah, and Acts (a curious combination), which can be dated with some confidence to about the middle of the fourth century, and another, not much later in

---

[1] An unpublished catalogue of Biblical papyri by Mr. P. L. Hedley enumerates 174 of the O.T. and 157 of the N.T., but most are very small and unimportant.

date, of the Gospel of St. John, excavated by Mr. Starkey (working under Mr. Guy Brunton) and now the property of the British and Foreign Bible Society. From these materials it has been possible for the Rev. G. Horner to reconstruct practically the whole of the Sahidic New Testament, an achievement of great value in view of the age and textual importance of this version.

Such was the position in 1930, when a discovery was made which threw all the others in the shade, and which is indeed only to be rivalled by that of the Codex Sinaiticus. This was the group of papyri now known as the Chester Beatty Biblical Papyri. The circumstances of the find have never been fully revealed; indeed they are known only to the natives who made it, and their statements, for obvious reasons, are not very dependable. The first reports spoke of the district of the Fayum, to the west of the Nile; but information given to Dr. Carl Schmidt was to the effect that the actual site was on the opposite side of the river, near the remains of the ancient city of Aphroditopolis. The papyri are said to have been found in a Coptic graveyard, enclosed in one or more jars, which is very probable, for other papyri have from time to time been similarly found, jars or buckets having been frequently used as receptacles for books in antiquity. They passed into the hands of dealers, and the bulk of the collection was acquired by Mr. A. Chester Beatty, a well-known American collector resident in England and the owner of a magnificent collection of illuminated manuscripts, both Western and Oriental. Some leaves and fragments, however, were acquired by the University of Michigan, and a few are in other hands; and it is quite possible that others may still turn up, since native discoverers are apt to divide their spoils, and dealers sometimes hold back a portion of a collection. As will be seen, some important additions have already been made to the find as originally announced.

The discovery was first notified by the present writer in an article in *The Times* of November 17, 1931. It was then described as consisting of portions of twelve manuscripts, of which eight contained books of the Old Testament, three of the New, while one contained some chapters of the apocryphal Book of Enoch and an unidentified Christian homily. The Old Testament group included (1) two substantial manuscripts of Genesis, one of the late third and the other of the early fourth century, covering between them the greater part of the book, and of especial value because both the Vaticanus and Sinaiticus are almost wholly lacking in this book; (2) a manuscript of Numbers and Deuteronomy, in a beautiful hand which cannot be later than the first half of the second century, of which portions (often very small) of 50 leaves have been preserved out of an original total of 108, with a large number of tiny fragments which it is difficult, if not impossible, to place; (3) a very fragmentary and tattered manuscript of Isaiah, finely written, apparently early in the third century, with a few marginal notes in Coptic; (4) one imperfect leaf (a portion of a second has since been identified) of Jeremiah, of the late second or early third century; (5) a manuscript of Ezekiel, Daniel, and Esther, originally described as two distinct manuscripts, but it is now clear that all the leaves belong to a single codex, though the Ezekiel is written in a different hand from the Daniel and Esther; it originally consisted of 118 leaves, of which 29 are in the Chester Beatty collection (8 each of Ezekiel and Esther, and 13 of Daniel), and 21 of Ezekiel, more perfect, in Princeton University Library; it was a tall, narrow volume, of which the lower third of each Chester Beatty leaf has been lost, in hands which may be assigned to the first half of the third century; (6) one leaf, and part of a second, of Ecclesiasticus, in a large, rough hand of the fourth century.

114

The New Testament books are of exceptional importance. One was originally a copy of all four Gospels and the Acts, written in a small hand which palæographers agree in assigning to the first half of the third century—that is to say, a century older than the Vaticanus and Sinaiticus. Portions of 30 leaves are preserved, out of an original total of 110; two are of Matthew, six of Mark, seven of Luke, two of John, and thirteen of Acts; but those of Matthew are almost negligible fragments, and those of Mark and Acts are small, though sufficient to be very useful. Some small fragments of this manuscript were among the Michigan acquisition, but were generously transferred to Mr. Beatty; and some scraps of Matthew, which combine with the Beatty fragments, are at Vienna. The second New Testament manuscript was originally announced as ten imperfect leaves of a codex of the Pauline Epistles, including portions of Romans, Philippians, Colossians, and 1 Thessalonians; but subsequent discoveries have greatly enlarged this description. First it was announced that the University of Michigan had acquired 30 leaves, in much more perfect condition, of the same manuscript, which were published in 1935 by Professor H. A. Sanders; and now it is permissible to announce that 46 more leaves, also in excellent

condition, have been secured by Mr. Beatty.
Therefore we now have, not merely a small portion,
but nearly the whole of a copy of the Epistles of
St. Paul, written in a fine hand which is not later
than the middle of the third century, and which the
foremost of then living papyrologists (Professor U.
Wilcken) would place about A.D. 200. Seven
leaves are missing at the beginning, and a corre-
sponding number (some of which may have been
blank) at the end, but otherwise only four leaves
(which one may hope have only been accidentally
separated, and may yet turn up) are wanting; so
that in all we have 86 leaves out of a total of 104.
The Pastoral Epistles do not seem to have been
included in the volume, for the missing leaves at
the end are not sufficient to contain them. Otherwise the collection is complete except for 2 Thessalonians, which must have occupied part of the
missing leaves; and it is noticeable that Hebrews
is placed immediately after Romans (an almost un-
precedented position), which shows that at the early
date when this manuscript was written no doubt
was felt as to its Pauline authorship. Through
the generous co-operation of the Michigan authorities, the whole was published together in 1936,
in a Supplement to the Beatty series, constituting a
notable addition to the textual apparatus of the

Epistles of St. Paul, in a copy written only about a century and a half after his death.

The third New Testament manuscript is 10 leaves (about one-third of the whole) of the book of Revelation, written in a rather rough hand, originally assigned to the second half of the third century, but which Wilcken would place in the first half, and perhaps near the beginning of it. In all, therefore, it will be seen that in these three papyrus manuscripts we have all the books of the New Testament, with the exception of the Pastoral and Catholic Epistles, represented more or less in copies which can be confidently assigned to the third century. A large part of the gap between the original writers and the earliest manuscripts which we possessed of them has thus been filled; and who knows what the future may still bring?

Finally, Mr. Beatty has eight leaves and two fragments, and the University of Michigan six leaves, of another manuscript, which contains the last eleven chapters of the Book of Enoch, here entitled "The Epistle of Enoch," and a Christian homily which Professor Campbell Bonner of Michigan has identified as the work of Melito of Sardis, who wrote in the second half of the second century. His name is plain to see in the papyrus, but the recognition of it is wholly due to Professor

Bonner. The Enoch portion of the manuscript gives us for the first time the original Greek text of Chapters 97–107 (Ch. 108, which is avowedly a different work, is not present). Before 1886 the book was only known (apart from a few quotations) in an Ethiopic translation. In that year a vellum manuscript was discovered at Akhmim in Egypt which contained the first 36 chapters of it in Greek, together with portions of the apocryphal Gospel and Apocalypse of Peter. The present discovery makes a very welcome addition to our knowledge of the book, which was very popular in ancient times, and is quoted in the Epistle of St. Jude. The papyrus is roughly written, by a scribe whose knowledge of Greek was very imperfect. This perhaps gives it a later appearance than its true date, and those who have studied it are inclined to place it in the fourth century. In recognition of the great courtesy of the University of Michigan in respect of the other manuscripts, the publication of Enoch and Melito has been left in the very capable hands of Professor Bonner (published 1937–40).

It will now be realized what an epoch-making addition to our knowledge of the history of the Bible has been made by this discovery. Instead of our evidence for the text of the Greek Bible beginning with the fourth century, we now have several wit-

nesses from the third century, and one even from
the beginning of the second. As already indicated
in Chapter III, we have learnt much of the way in
which books were written and circulated in the
second and third centuries, and a flood of new
light has been thrown on the condition of the text,
and especially of the Gospel text, during this previously dim period. Let us see what this new evidence amounts to, especially with regard to the
New Testament, and its bearing on the problems
and controversies which have been stated above.

Imperfect as the papyrus of the Gospels and Acts
is, there is enough, except in respect of Matthew,
to show what the general character of the text was.
Two points are clear at once: it does not align
itself wholly with either the Neutral or the Western
family, still less with the Byzantine; and its
character is not the same in all the books. Fuller
analysis of the various readings leads to the interesting conclusion that in Mark it quite definitely
shows more agreement with the Cæsarean group
(especially with the Washington Codex) than
with any other, and thus (considering its date)
reinforces the probability that the Cæsarean text
was extant in Egypt before Origen left that country.
In Luke and John the Cæsarean text has not yet
been identified, but the papyrus here comes closer

to the Neutral group, without, however, being by any means identical with it. Rather, it may be said to hold an intermediate position between the Neutral and Western groups, inclining to the Neutral side in Luke, and slightly to the Western in John. It has none of the more striking variants found in the more extreme Western authorities in Luke. In Acts it is distinctly nearer to the Neutral group than to the Western. It is interesting and significant to notice that while it contains several readings for which the evidence is mainly Western, or at any rate non-Neutral, it has none of the readings especially characteristic of the Western text, which are particularly numerous and noticeable in this book. The conclusions to be drawn from this will be considered in the final chapter.

With regard to the Pauline Epistles, final results cannot yet be given, since there has not been time fully to digest the new material which has so lately been added to our knowledge of this manuscript. It can, however, be stated with confidence that the character of the manuscript is fairly uniform throughout; that it agrees definitely with the Neutral group (which here includes the Alexandrinus as well as the Vaticanus and Sinaiticus) rather than with the Western (which is represented by the three Græco-Latin manuscripts known as

CHESTER BEATTY PAPYRUS I
Gospels and Acts, Third Century

ΠΡΟΣ ΚΟΡΙΝΘΙΟΥΣ Β

ΠΑΥΛΟΣΑΠΟΣΤΟΛΟΣΧΡΥ ΙΗΥ ΔΙΑΘΕΛΗ
ΜΑΤΟΣΘΥ ΚΑΙΤΕΙΜΟΘΕΟΣΟΑΔΕΛΦΟΣΤΗ
ΕΚΚΛΗΣΙΑΤΟΥΘΥ ΤΟΥΟΥΣΗΕΝΚΟΡΙΝΘΩ
ΣΥΝΤΟΙΣΑΓΙΟΙΣΠΑΣΙΝΤΟΙΣΟΥΣΙΝΕΝΟΛΗ
ΤΗΑΧΑΙΑΧΑΡΙΣΚΑΙΥΜΕΙΝΚΑΙΕΙΡΗΝΗ
ΑΠΟΘΥ ΠΑΤΡΟΣΗΜΩΝ ΚΑΙΚΥ ΙΗΥ ΧΡΥ
ΕΥΛΟΓΗΤΟΣΟΘΣ ΚΑΙΠΑΤΗΡΤΟΥΚΥ ΗΜΩ
ΙΗΥ ΧΡΥ ΟΠΑΤΗΡΤΩΝ ΟΙΚΤΕΙΡΜΩΝ
ΚΑΙΘΣ ΠΑΣΗΣΠΑΡΑΚΛΗΣΕΩΣΟΠΑΡΑ
ΚΑΛΩΝΗΜΑΣΕΠΙΠΑΣΗΤΗΘΛΕΙΨΕΙ
ΗΜΩΝ ΕΙΣΤΟΔΥΝΑΣΘΑΙΗΜΑΣΠΑΡΑ
ΚΑΛΕΙΝΤΟΥΣΕΝΠΑΣΗΘΛΕΙΨΕΙΔΙΑ
ΤΗΣΠΑΡΑΚΛΗΣΕΩΣ ΠΑΡΑΚΑΛΟΥ
ΜΕΘΑΑΥΤΟΙΥΠΟΤΟΥΘΥ ΟΤΙΘΩΣΠΕ
ΡΙΟΣΕΥΕΙΤΑΠΑΘΗΜΑΤΑΤΟΥΧΡΥ ΕΙΣ
ΗΜΑΣ ΟΥΤΩΣΔΙΑΤΟΥΧΡΥ ΠΕΡΙΣΣΕΥΕΙ
ΚΑΙΗΠΑΡΑΚΛΗΣΙΣ ΕΙΤΕΔΕΘΛΙΒΟΜΕΘ
ΘΑΥΠΕΡΤΗΣΥΜΩΝΠΑΡΑΚΛΗΣΕΩΣΚΑΙ
ΣΩΤΗΡΙΑΣ ΕΙΤΕ ΠΑΡΑΚΑΛΟΥΜΕΘΑΥΠΕ
ΙΗΣΥΜΩΝΠΑΡΑΚΛΗΣΕΩΣΤΗΣΕΝΕΡ
ΓΟΥΜΕΝΗΣΕΝΥΠΟΜΟΝΗΤΩΝΑΥΤΩ
ΠΑΘΗΜΑΤΩΝ ΟΥΤΩΚΑΙΗΠΟΤΑ
ΟΣ ΗΜΩΝ ΕΛΠΙΣΗΜΩΝ

CHESTER BEATTY PAPYRUS II
Pauline Epistles, Early Third Century

D, F, G); and that its agreement is greatest with the Vaticanus, and next to that with the Sinaiticus. One reading of special interest may be noted. There has always been some doubt as to the position of the doxology which in our ordinary texts stands at the end of Romans (xvi. 25-7). This is a case in which our "received text" does not represent the Byzantine text current in the Middle Ages; for the great mass of the minuscule manuscripts (and one uncial, L) have these verses at the end of chapter xiv. Erasmus, however, preferred here to follow the Vulgate, which agrees with the older Greek manuscripts. The Alexandrinus and a few other authorities have them in both places; which seems to represent a transitional stage in the transposition of the passage from one place to the other, or to show that it was sometimes read in one place and sometimes in the other. The Vaticanus, Sinaiticus, Claromontanus, and a few other manuscripts and the older versions have them at the end of chapter xvi. A few Western authorities (a corrector of the Claromontanus and the manuscripts F, G) have them in neither place. There was evidently some uncertainty about the two last chapters in ancient times, and the second-century heretic Marcion seems to have omitted them from his edition of the Pauline Epistles. These doubts have been revived by modern scholars, who especially find difficulties in chapter xvi, with its long list of greetings to individuals in a church which St. Paul had not then visited. Chapter xv is not easily separable from chapter xiv, and the internal arguments against its being an original part of the Epistle are not convincing; but chapter xvi is in any case of the nature of a postscript. It is therefore interesting to find that our papyrus inserts the doxology at the end of chapter xv, proceeding immediately to append the text of xvi. If any authority had previously been known which placed it in this position, it is likely that many scholars would have accepted it as correct, whether they regarded chapter xvi as a postscript or (as some think) as an originally quite distinct letter of introduction for Phœbe to the church at Ephesus. The absence of other support is the main reason which makes one hesitate to accept the evidence of this, the earliest extant authority for the Epistle; but it certainly adds a new element to a puzzling problem. Perhaps the most probable solution is that it was usual to read the doxology in church at the end of either xiv or xv, omitting (as of no edificatory interest) the long list of personal salutations in xvi.

Of the Revelation papyrus all that need be said

is that it ranges itself on the whole with the oldest of our previously known authorities, but is independent of all of them. The authorities for this book fall into three groups: (1) four uncial manuscripts, headed by the Sinaiticus and Alexandrinus (the Vaticanus is defective here); (2) a later uncial and about 40 minuscules, which seem to represent a revision; (3) the Byzantine text. The Beatty papyrus shows most agreements with the early uncials, and least with the Byzantine text; but in doubtful readings it disagrees more often than it agrees with each of them.

With regard to the Old Testament portion of the Beatty collection, since we are not dealing here with the Old Testament at any length, it may suffice to call attention to three points which show how important this part of the discovery is. In the first place it gives us by far the oldest text we have of the book of Genesis. The Vaticanus and Sinaiticus are deficient in this book, and we have hitherto had to depend mainly on the Alexandrinus of the fifth century. Now we have the two Beatty papyri, covering between them the greater part of the book; and to these has to be added yet another recent discovery, a very fragmentary papyrus at Berlin, probably of the early part of the fourth century, originally acquired in 1906 but not published till

1927.[1] Between these three papyri there is a marked affinity, and we now have a fairly secure foundation for the Septuagint text of this book.

Next, the papyrus of Numbers and Deuteronomy has the distinction of being the oldest extant manuscript of any part of the Bible in any language. Its discovery increases our hopes of the eventual discovery of other manuscripts of the second or even the first century. For the Old Testament it would be of the greatest assistance to have a manuscript of some book other than the Pentateuch (in which, as explained above, variations are fewer and less important) earlier than the time of Origen, whose well-meant labours did much to obscure the original form of the Greek version by incorporating the readings of the accepted Hebrew text; and for the New Testament it would go far towards solving the problems of the various families of text that have come down to us.

Thirdly, the papyrus of Daniel has a special interest, which can be briefly explained. In this book the Septuagint version differs markedly from the Hebrew, and there is evidence that it gave dissatisfaction at a very early date. It was accordingly superseded by a new translation, based upon the

---

[1] By C. Schmidt and H. A. Sanders (*University of Michigan Studies*).

Hebrew text as established after A.D. 100, made by Theodotion (see p. 18 above) in the second half of the second century; and so effectively was it replaced that it has survived only in a single late Greek manuscript and in a Syriac translation. It is therefore a real contribution to knowledge to find that the Beatty papyrus has the original Septuagint version, for which it supplies us, for a large part of the book, with evidence perhaps a thousand years older than our only other Greek witness, and enables us to check the value of the latter's evidence. So far as appears from a first examination, it seems (as one would expect from its date) to be independent of the influence of Origen.

Such are, in brief summary, the contents and character of the Chester Beatty papyri. They are indeed a momentous discovery, affecting alike the Old Testament, the New Testament, and the non-canonical literature of the Church. They have carried back the evidences of our faith by a century, they have given us specimens of the volumes of the Gospels and of the Pauline Epistles which were in use among the Christians of the third century, and they give us an insight into the manner in which the text of the sacred books was handed down through the ages of persecution. Other discoveries may yet be made—indeed some, not so directly affecting the Bible text, have already been reported; but these are sufficient to make our generation remarkable in Bible history. It remains to make an attempt to sum up the conclusions to which all the discoveries of the last fifty years seem to point.

Since this book was first in type, two interesting discoveries have been announced. One is a small fragment of a papyrus codex containing parts of John xviii. 31–3, 37, 38, of the first half of the second century, discovered by Mr. C. H. Roberts among the papyri in the John Rylands Library at Manchester. It is the earliest extant fragment of the New Testament, and is a conclusive proof of the early date of the Fourth Gospel. The other consists of portions of three leaves of a papyrus codex of a hitherto unknown Gospel, with close similarities in phrase with the Synoptic Gospels and St. John. This (which is in the British Museum, and has been edited by H. I. Bell and T. C. Skeat) also is of the first half of the second century. Either it is one of the narratives to which St. Luke refers in his preface, or, if it is based upon the canonical Gospels, it is a proof of the early date of all of them, including the Fourth, which must certainly belong to the first century.

CHAPTER X

THE POSITION TO-DAY

IN Chapter VII the position reached in 1881 was described, which was crystallized in the Revised Version of the New Testament and Westcott and Hort's edition of the Greek text. How has this been affected by the discoveries of the last fifty years, described in the last two chapters, culminating in the Chester Beatty papyri?

As explained previously, the immediate result of the controversy of 1881 was to eliminate the "received" or Byzantine text which had dominated Christianity for over a millennium. Scholars were agreed that this represented the results of a long process of revision, beginning about the end of the fourth century, and characterized by an attempt at uniformity of phrase, the removal of obscurities, the harmonization of alternative versions, and similar editorial handiwork. They were agreed that it was necessary to look further back, to the earliest manuscripts and versions, and to such later authorities as might seem more or less to have escaped the prevalent tendency to revision. These earlier authorities fell, according to the views of 1881, into two main groups, labelled respectively "Neutral," which meant the group headed by the Vaticanus and Sinaiticus, and "Western," which meant everything that was pre-Byzantine and non-Neutral, but of which the outstanding representatives (as showing the greatest amount of divergence from the other types of text) were the Codex Bezæ and the Old Latin version. The great problem therefore was, which of these families comes nearest to the original form of the New Testament books? And every new discovery was scrutinized to see what bearing it had upon this problem.

At first, as indicated at the beginning of Chapter VIII, the current ran rather in favour of the Westerners. When the Old Syriac version was brought to light, attention was concentrated on its divergences from the Neutral text; and as everything which was not Neutral was classed as Western, it was regarded as a reinforcement of the Western camp. Similarly a good deal of the Washington codex could be claimed as non-Neutral; and Families 1 and 13 appeared to be associated with the Syriac versions. Further, the small discoveries of Biblical papyri which were made from time to time in Egypt before 1930 were certainly not all Neutral; and examination of the writings of the early Fathers tended to strengthen the proof that most of them used non-Neutral texts. In short, the general tendency was to weaken the position of exclusive superiority claimed by Westcott and Hort for the Neutral text, by showing that it was at any rate of restricted circulation, and that it had rivals of at least equal age.

But it was one thing to make some abatement in the claims of the Neutral text; it was quite another to put the Western in its place. The progress of discovery and examination showed that the problem was not so simple as this. The fact was that the more the number of non-Neutral authorities increased, the less possible it became to group them all together as a single family under the name of Western. They were not Western, for they were found in Syria and Egypt, indeed throughout the Christian world; and they were not a family, for they differed too much among themselves. People talked lightly of the Old Latin and Old Syriac as being Western authorities; but in point of fact they differ from one another more than they do from the Neutral. In 27 passages in which important various readings are found, the Sinaitic

Syriac agrees 16 times with the Vaticanus and only 5 times with Codex Bezæ; it agrees only 5 times with the Old Latin, while it disagrees 17 times. On balance, therefore, it would be more true to reckon the Old Syriac as an ally of the Neutral than of the text which can truly be described as Western. It may be added, moreover, that the Syriac and Latin witnesses do not even agree among themselves. In 7 cases the two Old Syriac manuscripts take different sides, and in 5 the Old Latin evidence is divided.

Similarly with the Old Coptic (Sahidic) version, which used to be regarded as, in part at least, an ally of the Western group. Discoveries in Egypt have greatly increased our knowledge of this version, and show that, while it contains a perceptible proportion of non-Neutral readings, it is far more a supporter of the Neutral text than of the true Western. Thus in 33 passages (substantially the same as those examined for the Old Syriac text), the Sahidic agrees 28 times with the Vaticanus and 24 times with the Sinaiticus, as against 7 times each with Codex Bezæ and the Old Latin. In 7 other cases the Old Latin authorities are divided.

Next we have to take into account the emergence of the Cæsarean family. Here discovery and study have co-operated to isolate a group of authorities who are neither Neutral nor Western, though they may at times agree with one or other of them. Their association with Origen proves that the text contained in them is of early date, which circulated, as we have good reason to believe, in Egypt, Palestine and Syria. If it is a proof that the Neutral text was not dominant in the East, it is equally a proof that not all non-Neutral early readings are to be classed as Western, and they do nothing to support the more characteristic variants of that type.

Thus while the discoveries of the last fifty years have shaken the exclusive predominance which Westcott and Hort assigned to the Vaticanus-Sinaiticus text, they have shattered to pieces the unity of the so-called Western text. In place of these two families, with the somewhat shadowy " Alexandrian " text, as envisaged by the two Cambridge scholars, we now seem to find our pre-Byzantine authorities falling into at least five categories; (1) the Vaticanus-Sinaiticus group, with its home in Egypt, and almost certainly in Alexandria, since it is difficult to imagine such splendid manuscripts being produced except in a great capital; it is a group obviously of great importance, being headed by these two outstanding manuscripts, supported by a number of early though fragmentary uncials and a few minuscules, and by the Bohairic and generally the Sahidic version, and to it the name *Alexandrian* may more appropriately, and with less appearance of begging the question, be applied than that of Neutral; (2) the true *Western* group, headed by the Codex Bezæ, the other Græco-Latin uncials, and the Old Latin version, especially in that earliest form of it which appears to be associated with Africa and to have been used by Cyprian; (3) the *Syriac* group, represented mainly by the Old Syriac version and the other versions (Georgian, Armenian) which appear to have been derived from it; (4) the *Cæsarean* group, as yet not fully worked out, but which may in part be extracted, as described above, from the Chester Beatty papyrus, the Washington and Koridethi codices, and Families 1 and 13, with the quotations in some of the works of Origen and Eusebius; and (5) a residue of unassorted readings, found in early authorities, but which it is quite inadmissible to claim as "Western" now that we realize that not everything that is not Neutral is Western.

It is, I think, just this unassorted residue that gives us the clue to the early history of the text of the New Testament. It is not always realized how unique were the conditions under which these books circulated in the early centuries. The ordinary works of classical literature were freely copied by professional scribes, and it is probable that the tradition of their text has come down to us mainly through the great libraries and the book-producing firms of capital cities. Even the books of the Greek Old Testament must for the most part have descended through untrammelled channels, except so far as they may have become involved in the fortunes of Christian literature. But the Christian books, before the recognition of Christianity by Constantine, were produced and circulated without the assistance of great libraries or a regular trade. Scholars need to apply the increased knowledge which we now possess of this period to the problems of the New Testament text, and to use both imagination and common sense in interpreting them.

The New Testament was not produced as a single work issued by an authoritative Church for the instruction of its members. The four Gospels were composed in different times and places over perhaps a third of a century, and for a time circulated separately among a number of other narratives of our Lord's life (of which the newly discovered fragment of an unknown Gospel may have been one). The Epistles were letters, or treatises in the form of letters, addressed to different congregations and only gradually made known to other Churches. The book of Revelation was an isolated production, which for a long time was not universally accepted. There was no central body to say what books were to be regarded as authoritative, or to supply certified copies of them. The apostles were scattered, and even the leaders of the Church in Jerusalem had neither the power nor the means to impose uniformity.

In these circumstances, we must imagine the literature of Christianity as spreading gradually, irregularly, and in a manner which made variations inevitable. In the earliest days, while the generation that had known our Lord on earth was alive, and while His second coming was expected in the immediate future, there would have been little demand for written records. But as the promise of His coming was delayed, and as the faith spread beyond the range of those who had known Him, the narratives which we now know came into being, together with many which have long ago disappeared. But not every congregation would have possessed a complete set of the books of their faith. One church might possess only one Gospel, another two or three or the complete four. A village or provincial town where there was a Christian congregation might hear that its neighbour had a copy of a book unknown to them, and might send and get a copy of it—made, very likely, by a copyist of more zeal than skill. Exact verbal accuracy of transcription was, after all, of little account. The Gospels were not thought of as works of literature. People were not concerned with the literary reputation of Matthew or Mark, but with the substance of their records of our Lord's life. They did not have to respect their actual words, as they would if they were transcribing the works of Thucydides or Plato. Rather a scribe might have thought he was doing good service if he smoothed away difficulties of phrase, if he made the narrative of one Evangelist conform with that of another, if he inserted proper names or pronouns for the sake of greater clearness, if he used a conventional form of words instead of an unusual one, even if he inserted a new incident into the narrative. Edification was the object, not literary exactitude.

In these circumstances, is it surprising if in the first two centuries a large number of minor variations, and some of greater magnitude, found their way into the copies of the Scripture which circulated in the towns and villages of Palestine, Syria, Egypt, Asia Minor, Italy, Africa, and even farther afield ? Rather we have to be thankful that greater and more serious corruption did not creep in. It is indeed a striking proof of the essential soundness of the tradition that with all these thousands of copies, tracing their ancestry back to so many different parts of the earth and to conditions of such diverse kinds, the variations of text are so entirely questions of detail, not of essential substance. For the main substance we may be content even with the latest copies which have handed down to us the ecclesiastical text of the Middle Ages. But if we wish to read the sacred books of our religion in a form as like as can be to that in which they were originally composed, we must endeavour to realize the conditions under which they were produced, and which we have been trying to describe.

We see therefore at first an uncontrolled, or imperfectly controlled, welter of variants, due to the errors of scribes or to well-meant editorial efforts. But naturally, as time went on, the leaders of the Church in different localities, or scholars who seriously studied and expounded the Christian religion, would be led to try to introduce order into the confusion, to revise the texts current in their neighbourhood, and to select what seemed to be the preferable form among two or more variants that offered themselves. The period of editorial labour and of scholarly study gradually came into existence. But this would at first be local effort and of limited effect. There was still no authoritative centre for the whole world, and Christianity was still at times a persecuted faith. There were times, no doubt, when the Christian books could be copied and read without serious hindrance. But there were also times when Christianity was actively persecuted and when, as we know from the records of the early Church, the sacred books were a special object of search and destruction. Official copies would at such times be especially exposed to danger.

It would therefore be natural if somewhat different forms of text came into existence in different parts of the Christian world, and if, along with them, there were a multitude of copies which conformed with no particular form. Scholars like Origen knew that there were great varieties of readings, and selected those which they regarded as the best. But it was not until Christianity was a recognized and authorized religion in the Roman Empire that editorial work could go on unimpeded. Even then there was no guarantee of uniformity. Different editors might work on different principles. Some would have as their main object the removal of difficulties in the way of ready comprehension by the ordinary reader. They would supply pronouns and names, they would use the phrases which by that time had become habitual, they would make slight grammatical alterations in accordance with current usage, they would avoid phrases which might give offence, and where alternative readings could be amalgamated they would be inclined to do so. Their object would be the edification of the reader by the presentation of an easily comprehensible text. On such principles such a text as the Byzantine text might be brought into being, and win its way to general acceptance in the Church at large.

Others, with bolder and more enterprising minds, might prefer to incorporate the more singular readings which they found in their authorities, and to handle the text more freely. Additions from various sources (such as the passages added in Codex Bezæ at Matt. xx. 28 and Luke vi. 5, or in the Washington Codex at Mark xvi. 14) would be welcome, and the editor might even feel free (as in Codex Bezæ in the Acts) to make extensive alterations due to his special knowledge. In such a way might arise that type of text which is found in Codex Bezæ and the Old Latin, to which the name of Western may properly be given.

Others, again, might simply do their best with the materials that lay to their hand, without any special principle either of exclusion or inclusion or harmonization, and so produce a text which would include readings that are found elsewhere in various types of text. Syria was a very definite province of the Christian Church, and might very naturally develop a local form of text; and so we find in the Old Syriac a text including many unquestionably early readings, some of which occur also in the Western group and others in the Neutral (or, as we prefer to call it, Alexandrian). It is a valuable witness, all the more because it incorporates elements of different types. Later, when Bishop Rabbula in the early fifth century undertook a revision of the texts then circulating in his diocese, he brought them more into conformity with the Byzantine type, then acquiring dominance in the Church, and so produced the Peshitta, which became the generally "received text" of Syrian Christianity.

Then again there would be texts produced by scholars in accordance with such principles of textual criticism as they had acquired. Of these we have an outstanding example in St. Jerome's revision of the Latin Bible which produced what we know as the Vulgate. Jerome was a trained scholar, who about A.D. 382 was invited by Pope

Damasus to undertake a revision of the Latin Bible, of which many discordant forms were then in circulation. He did so with reference to the oldest and best Greek manuscripts he could find, most of which seem to have belonged to what we have called the Alexandrian family. Indeed, the Codex Sinaiticus is the Greek manuscript which most conspicuously agrees with the Vulgate. Jerome, however, more cautious than our own Revisers, was sparing in his alterations; he tells us himself that he often left passages untouched which he might have corrected, in order to preserve the familiar form, and only made changes where he thought them material. On these lines he dealt with the Gospels. The Epistles (where the existing variations were fewer) he revised only very slightly; and for the Old Testament, instead of revising it from the Septuagint, as originally proposed by the Pope, he eventually made a fresh translation from the Hebrew.

Jerome's revision of the Gospels is thus a good example of how a scholar in the fourth century might set to work; and in the case of the Greek Old Testament we know of no less than three scholars who in the third century undertook a similar task. The first of these was Origen himself, who produced his colossal edition of the Septuagint in six parallel columns (and hence known as the Hexapla) containing the Hebrew text as then accepted by Jewish scholars, the same in Greek characters, the translations of Aquila, Symmachus, and Theodotion, and his own revision of the Septuagint, in which he endeavoured to bring it into conformity with the Hebrew. Origen's edition was separately issued by his disciples, Eusebius and Pamphilus, and has had a great, but rather unfortunate, effect on the history of the Septuagint text, since the original Greek has been somewhat obscured by his conformation of it to the Hebrew. Other editions of the Septuagint were produced by Lucian of Antioch and Hesychius of Alexandria; and these three editions seem to have circulated respectively in Palestine, in Syria and Constantinople, and in Egypt. The practice, therefore, of scholarly revision and of local texts is well evidenced in the case of the Greek Old Testament, and it is perfectly natural to suppose that the same was the case with the New. Some scholars have indeed, on the strength of an observation of Jerome which does not seem to authorize so far-reaching a deduction, supposed that Lucian and Hesychius also produced editions of the New Testament, and that these are reflected in our Byzantine and Alexandrian families. Whether they, or other scholars unknown

141

to us, did so is immaterial for our present purpose. The point is that the early dissemination of various readings and scholarly revision of them are proved facts in relation to the Latin Bible and the Greek Old Testament, and may fairly be presumed in the case of the Greek New Testament.

To such revision it seems reasonable to attribute our Cæsarean and Alexandrian families. The aim of the scholarly editor is not to produce the easiest text for the reader, but to get as near as he can to the original text of the author. Where alternative readings exist he will therefore tend to choose the harder rather than the easier, the shorter rather than the longer, the reading that differs from that in another Gospel rather than one which coincides; because, if alteration has taken place, it is likely to have been in the direction of the easier, longer, and harmonized readings. Such seems in particular to be the character of the Alexandrian text. It is, on the whole, a shorter and more austere text than the others. The Cæsarean text has not yet been fully established, and it is too soon to draw final conclusions about it; but it also seems to show signs of scholarly method rather than of general inclusiveness or colourless handling in the interests of the reader. We may not always agree with the editor's choice; but it has to be remembered that

142

he was working with manuscripts earlier than any which we now possess.

The general conclusion to which we seem to be led is that there is no royal road to the recovery of the original text of the New Testament. Fifty years ago it seemed as if Westcott and Hort had found such a road, and that we should depart from the Codex Vaticanus (except in the case of obvious scribal blunders) at our peril. The course both of discoveries and of critical study has made it increasingly difficult to believe that the Vaticanus and its allies represent a stream of tradition that has come down practically uncontaminated from the original sources. Based as they must have been on a multitude of different rolls, it would have been a singularly happy accident if all had been of the same character, and all deriving without contamination from the originals. The uniformity of character which on the whole marks the Vaticanus and Sinaiticus is better to be explained as the result of skilled editing of well-selected authorities on a definite principle. Therefore, while respecting the authority due to the age and character of this recension, we shall be disposed to give more consideration than Westcott and Hort did to other early readings which found a home in the Western, Syriac, or Cæsarean texts, but we may still believe (though here personal predilections come into play, and others may take different views) that the Alexandrian text gives us on the whole the nearest approximation to the original form of the sacred books.

In this short survey of a great subject, we have endeavoured to give in simple language an outline of the general history of the Bible text, an account of the many discoveries which have modified and extended our knowledge of it, and an indication of the conclusions to which scholarly opinion seems to be tending. It is a fascinating story to those who care for their Bible. It is the life-history of the greatest of books, diversified by interesting episodes which appeal to our human sympathies; and we venture to think that the result is reassuring. It may be disturbing to some to part with the conception of a Bible handed down through the ages without alteration and in unchallenged authority; but it is a higher ideal to face the facts, to apply the best powers with which God has endowed us to the solution of the problems which they present to us; and it is reassuring at the end to find that the general result of all these discoveries and all this study is to strengthen the proof of the authenticity of the Scriptures, and our conviction that we have in our hands, in substantial integrity, the veritable Word of God.

144

APPENDIX I

THE PRINCIPAL MANUSCRIPTS AND VERSIONS OF THE GREEK BIBLE

(WITH THE SYMBOLS BY WHICH THEY ARE KNOWN)

OLD TESTAMENT (SEPTUAGINT)

א or S. *Codex* [1] *Sinaiticus*, 4th cent.; 43 leaves at Leipzig, 3 fragments at Leningrad, and 199 leaves in the British Museum. Discovered by Tischendorf in the monastery of St. Catherine at Mount Sinai, 1844 and 1859; at St. Petersburg, 1859–1933. Contains fragments of Gen. xxiii. and xxiv. and of Num. v.–vii., 1 Chr. ix. 27–xix. 17, 2 Esd. ix. 9–end, Esth., Tob., Jud., 1 and 4 Macc., Isa., Jer., Lam. i. 1–ii. 20, Joel, Obad., Jon., Nah., Hab., Zeph., Hag., Zech., Mal., Psalms, Prov., Eccles., Cant., Wisd., Ecclus., Job, (besides whole N.T. on 148 leaves, see below). Many corrections, some said to have been taken from a manuscript (qu. at Cæsarea ?) corrected by Pamphilus. Four columns to the page (2 in the poetical books).

A. *Codex Alexandrinus*, 5th cent., in British Museum; complete (O.T. and N.T.), except for loss of Ps. xlix. 19–lxxix. 10 and a few verses in Gen. xiv–xvi. and 1 Kings xii.–xiv.; 3 and 4 Macc. are included. Presented by Cyril Lucar, Patriarch of

---

[1] The term Codex means a manuscript in modern book form of quires and pages as opposed to a roll, but it is in practice specially applied to old uncial manuscripts, particularly of the Bible.

Constantinople, to Charles I in 1627, and transferred by George II to British Museum in 1757. Two columns to the page.

B. *Codex Vaticanus*, 4th cent., in Vatican Library since at least 1481; complete (O.T. and N.T.), except for loss of Gen. i. 1–xlvi. 28, Ps. cv. 27–cxxxvii. 6, and a few verses of 2 Sam. ii. Macc. was never included. Three columns to the page.

C. *Codex Ephraemi*, 5th cent.; 64 palimpsest leaves of O.T. (with 145 of N.T.), in Bibliothèque Nationale at Paris. Contains portions of Job, Prov., Eccles., Wisdom, Ecclus., Cant. One column to the page.

D. *Cotton Genesis*, 5th cent., with illustrations, in British Museum. Acquired by Sir R. Cotton; almost wholly destroyed by fire in 1731, but text known from collations made previously.

E. *Bodleian Genesis*, 10th cent., at Oxford; continued in minuscule manuscripts at Leningrad and the British Museum.

F. *Codex Ambrosianus*, 5th cent., in Ambrosian Library at Milan. Contains Gen. xxxi. 15–Jos. xii. 12. Three columns to the page.

G. *Codex Sarravianus,* 5th cent.; 130 leaves at Leyden, 22 at Paris, 1 at Leningrad. Contains portions of Pentateuch, Jos. and Judges, in text of Origen's Hexapla, with Origen's marks of additions and omissions, but only imperfectly. Two columns to the page.

Q. *Codex Marchalianus*, 6th cent., in Vatican Library. Contains the Prophets, with Hexaplar readings and Origen's marks added in the margin. One column to the page.

Θ. *Washington Codex*, 6th cent., in Freer Museum at Washington. Contains Deut. and Jos., except for loss of Deut. v. 16–vi. 18 and Jos. iii. 3–iv. 10. Originally contained all Hexateuch, perhaps Octateuch. Two columns to the page.

911. *Berlin Papyrus*, 4th cent., in Staatsbibliothek at Berlin. Contains portions of Gen. i. 16–xxv. 8. One column to the page.

961. *Chester Beatty Papyrus IV*, 4th cent. Contains Gen. ix. 1–xv. 14, xvii. 7–xliv. 22, with mutilations. Two columns to the page.

146

962. *Chester Beatty Papyrus V*, late 3rd cent. Contains Gen. viii. 13–ix. 1, xxiv. 13–xxv. 21, xxx. 24–xxxv. 16, xxxix. 4–xlvi. 33, with mutilations. One column to the page.

963. *Chester Beatty Papyrus VI*, early 2nd cent. Contains portions of Num. v. 12–viii. 19, xiii, xxv.5–xxxvi. 13, Deut. i. 20–xii. 17, xviii, xix, xxvii. 6–xxxiv. 12. Two columns to the page.

967, 968. *Chester Beatty Papyri IX, X*, early 3rd cent. Contains Ezek. xi. 25–xxxix. 29, Dan. iii. 72–viii. 27, Esther ii. 20–viii. 6, with considerable lacunæ. Ezek. is by a different scribe. Dan. is the version of Septuagint, elsewhere only preserved in Codex Chisianus.

PRINCIPAL VERSIONS

LATIN:

(a) *Old Latin,* 2nd cent.; fragments only, except of Apocrypha (but greater part of Gen.–Judges in Lyons Heptateuch).

(b) *Vulgate,* late 4th cent.; Psalter (in two versions, known as Roman and Gallican) and Job translated by Jerome from Septuagint, and all the books of the Hebrew Canon from Hebrew. Principal manuscripts, codices Turonensis (Gen.–Num., 6th–7th cent.), Ottobonianus (Gen.–Judges, 7th cent.), Amiatinus (O.T., early 8th cent.), Cavensis (O.T., 9th cent.), Theodulfianus (O.T., 9th cent.), Vallicellianus (O.T., 9th cent.).

SYRIAC:

(a) *Peshitta,* early 5th cent.

(b) *Syro-Hexaplar,* a Syriac translation, made about A.D. 616 by Paul of Tella, of Origen's edition of the Septuagint in his Hexapla, with Origen's marks. The principal authority for Origen's work.

COPTIC:

(a) *Sahidic,* 2nd and 3rd cent.; complete manuscripts of Lev., Num., Deut., 1 and 2 Sam., Psa., Isaiah, Jonah; considerable portions of poetical books; fragments of others.

(b) *Bohairic,* 3rd–4th cent.; Pentateuch, Prophets, Psalms, Job.

NEW TESTAMENT

ℵ. *Codex Sinaiticus*, 4th cent.; see above. N.T. on 148 leaves, complete, with Epistle of Barnabas and Shepherd of Hermas, Vis. i. 1–Mand. iv. 6.

A. *Codex Alexandrinus*, 5th cent.; see above. N.T., with Epistles of Clement (2 Clem. incomplete) and Psalms of Solomon (lost) at end; Mt. i. 1–xxv. 6, Jn. vi. 50–viii. 52, 2 Cor. iv. 13–xii. 6, 1 Clem. lvii. 7–lxiii. 4, 2 Clem. xii. 5 to end, missing.

B. *Codex Vaticanus*, 4th cent.; see above. N.T., imperfect at end, lacking Heb. ix. 14 to end, Pastoral Epistles, and Revelation.

C. *Codex Ephraemi*, 5th cent.; see above. 145 leaves of N.T. (out of original 238), including portions of every book except 2 Thess. and 2 John, but none complete.

D. *Codex Bezæ*, 5th cent. (?), in Cambridge University Library (presented by Theodore Beza in 1581). Contained Gospels, Acts, and Catholic Epistles, but Acts xxii. 29–end and all Cath. except 3 Jn. 11–15 are lost, with other mutilations. A Græco-Latin manuscript with Greek and Latin on opposite pages. Text written in sense-lines.

D₂. *Codex Claromontanus*, 6th cent., in Bibliothèque Nationale at Paris. Belonged (like D) to Beza. Contains Pauline Epistles. Græco-Latin manuscript, with text in sense-lines.

E₂. *Codex Laudianus*, 7th cent., in Bodleian Library at Oxford (presented by Laud in 1636). Græco-Latin manuscript of Acts, with Latin and Greek (in that order) on opposite pages, in very short sense-lines. Used by Bede.

W. *Codex Washingtonensis*, late 4th or 5th cent., in Freer Museum at Washington Contains Gospels. See above, pp. 100–2.

Θ. *Codex Koridethianus*, 9th cent. (?), at Tiflis. Contains Gospels. See above, p. 104.

046. *Codex Vaticanus 2066*, 8th cent., sometimes known as B₂. Contains Revelation, and is the head of a large group of minuscule manuscripts of that book.

P⁴⁵. *Chester Beatty Papyrus I*, early 3rd cent. Portions of 30 leaves, out of original 110, of papyrus codex of Gospels and Acts. See above, p. 115.

P⁴⁶. *Chester Beatty Papyrus II,* early 3rd cent. 86 leaves (56 in Beatty collection in London, 30 at University of Michigan), out of original 104, of papyrus codex of Pauline Epistles. Pastoral Epp. apparently not included, and 2 Thess. lost, with Rom. i. 1–v. 17 and other mutilations. See above, pp. 115–6.

P⁴⁷. *Chester Beatty Papyrus III,* late 3rd cent. 10 leaves, out of original 32, of papyrus codex of Revelation. Contains Rev. ix. 10–xvii. 2, with mutilations. See above, p. 117.

Family 1. The group of minuscules known by the numbers 1, 118, 131, 209. See above, p. 103.

Family 13. The group of minuscules known by the numbers 13, 69, 124, 346; to which 211, 543, 713, 788, 826, 828 have affinities. See above, p. 102.

Minuscule 33, 9th cent., in Bibliothèque Nationale at Paris. A minuscule of Gospels, Acts and Epistles with a very good text, akin to that of B.

Minuscule 81, A.D. 1044, in British Museum. Contains Acts, in a very good text.

PRINCIPAL VERSIONS

LATIN:

(a) Old Latin, 2nd cent. Two main classes, known as (i) African, represented chiefly by the manuscripts *k, e, m* (Speculum) and quotations in Cyprian and Priscillian, (ii) European, represented chiefly by the manuscripts *a, b* and many others, but with considerable divergences among themselves.

(b) Vulgate, made by Jerome, A.D. 382–4. The Gospels revised from O.L., with reference to Greek manuscripts mainly of Alexandrian type; other books much more slightly revised. Principal manuscripts, Amiatinus, Cavensis, Fuldensis, Sangermanensis, Lindisfarnensis, Vallicellianus.

SYRIAC:

(a) Old Syriac, 2nd cent. Represented only by two imperfect manuscripts of the Gospels, the Sinaitic (4th or 5th cent.) and the Curetonian (5th cent.)

(b) Peshitta, made by Rabbula, about A.D. 411. The accepted version of the Syrian Church. Complete N.T., except 2 Peter,

2 and 3 John, Jude, and Revelation, which the Syrian Church did not accept. Many manuscripts, from 5th cent. onwards.

COPTIC:

(*a*) *Sahidic*, 2nd–3rd cent. Complete manuscripts of John, Acts, Revelation, and many fragments, covering whole N.T., 4th–5th cent., with complete copies of most books, 9th cent. and later.

(*b*) *Bohairic*, 3rd–4th cent. The accepted version of the Coptic Church. Many manuscripts, from A.D. 889 onwards.

FATHERS:

The most important patristic quotations are those in Irenæus (*c*. 135–202), Clement of Alexandria (*c*. 155–220), Origen (185–253), Tertullian (*c*. 150–220), Hippolytus (fl. *c*. 220), Cyprian (*c*. 200–258), Eusebius (*c*. 270–340), Aphraates (Syrian, fl. *c*. 340), Ephraem (Syrian, *ob*. 378), Chrysostom (*c*. 347–407), Jerome (*c*. 345–420), Augustine (354–430), Priscillian (*ob*. 385).

APPENDIX II

THE PEDIGREE OF THE NEW TESTAMENT TEXT

THE following is an attempt to illustrate in tabular form the history of the Bible text. It must be emphasized, however, that no table can represent the infinite complexity of the descent, caused by the interaction of various groups, the sporadic revisions of editors and scribes, etc. It does, however, show the main facts, viz. that our common Greek texts and the Authorized Version represent the latest manuscripts of a late revision, gradually formed in the Byzantine Church about the fourth to the eighth centuries; that our revised Greek texts and the Revised Version derive from the earliest manuscripts and the earliest Versions, in which the earliest editions of the text were embodied; and that behind these lies a period before these earliest types of text were formed, and during which they were taking shape.

150

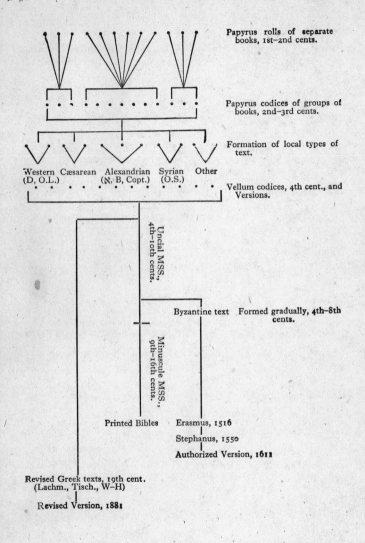

Papyrus rolls of separate
books, 1st–2nd cents.

Papyrus codices of groups of
books, 2nd–3rd cents.

Formation of local types of
text.

Western Cæsarean Alexandrian Syrian Other
(D, O.L.)   (א, B, Copt.)   (O.S.)

Vellum codices, 4th cent., and
Versions.

Uncial MSS.,
4th–10th cents.

Byzantine text   Formed gradually, 4th–8th
cents.

Minuscule MSS.,
9th–16th cents.

Printed Bibles   Erasmus, 1516

Stephanus, 1550

Authorized Version, 1611

Revised Greek texts, 19th cent.
(Lachm., Tisch., W–H)

Revised Version, 1881

INDEX

Alexandrian text of N.T., 82;
and see s.v. Neutral

Antwerp Polyglot, 59

Aristides, Apology of, 89

Assyria, libraries of, 9

Authorised Version, 51 ff.

Babylonia, books in, 9, 10

Bengel, J. A., classification of
MSS., 66

Bentley, R., 61, 64

Bishops' Bible (English), 51

Bohairic (Coptic) Version, 41,
147, 150

Bonner, Prof. Campbell, 117,
118

Books, form of, in classical
period, 23 ff.

Burgon, Dean, 87

Byzantine text of N.T., 39,
65, 92, 127, 137

Cæsarean text of Gospels, 106,
130, 142

Chester Beatty papyri, 14,
28 f., 112 ff.

Classical authors, earliest
MSS. of, 33

Classification of MSS.; by
Bengel, 66; by Semler,
66; by Griesbach, 67;
by Westcott and Hort,
82 ff.; a new classifica-
tion, 131 f.

Codex form of book, in vellum, 24 ff.; in papyrus,
27 ff.

Codices: for individual codices, see s.v. Manuscripts

Complutensian Polyglot, 43,
59

Constantine, effect on Bible of
his acceptance of Chris-
tianity, 38

Coptic Versions of Bible, 35,
41, 147, 150

Coverdale, M., English Bible
of, 49; editor of Great
Bible, 50

153

Cureton, W., 90
Curetonian Syriac MS., 90
Cursive writing, 27

Daniel, Chester Beatty papyrus of, 114, 124, 147
Deuteronomy, Chester Beatty papyrus of, 114, 124, 146; Coptic Papyrus of, 111
Diatessaron, of Tatian, 31, 94–8
Dura, fragment of *Diatessaron* found at, 96

Ecclesiasticus, Chester Beatty fragments of, 114
Egypt, early books in, 10
English Bible, 47–54
Enoch, Book of, 31, 117 f.
Erasmus, Greek N.T. of, 44
Esther, Chester Beatty papyrus of, 114, 147
Estienne, R. *See* Stephanus
Ezekiel, Chester Beatty papyrus of, 114, 147

Family 1 of Gospels MSS., 103, 132, 149
Family 13 of Gospels MSS., 102, 132, 149
Fathers, quotations in, 60, 67, 83, 92, 150
Fell, Dr. J., 60
Ferrar Group of Gospels MSS. *See* Family 13

Freer, C. L., Bible MSS. of, 98 ff.

Genesis: Berlin papyrus, 123, 146; Bodleian MS., 146; Chester Beatty papyri, 113, 123, 146; Cotton MS., 146
Geneva Bible (English), 50
Georgian Version, 107
Gibson, Mrs., 90
Gospels and Acts, Chester Beatty papyrus of, 29, 115, 119 f., 148
Great Bible (English), 50
Griesbach, J. J., classification of MSS., 67

Harris, J. Rendel, 89
Hebrew, earliest writings in, 10
Hebrew Old Testament, earliest MSS. of, 11; formation of Canon, 12
Hebrews, Epistle to, papyrus of, 110
Hedley, P. L., catalogue of Biblical papyri, 111 n.
Hesychius, edition of Septuagint, 141
Hexapla, of Origen, 18, 141, 147
Horner, G., edition of Sahidic N.T., 112

Isaiah, Chester Beatty papyrus of, 114

James I, influence on Authorised Version, 51
Jeremiah, Chester Beatty fragments of, 114
Jerome, St., and the Vulgate, 139 f.

Koridethi Codex of Gospels, 104, 132, 148

Lachmann, C., edition of N.T., 69 ff.
Lake, Prof. K., 77, 103, 106, 107
Legg, S. C. E., edition of N.T., 81
Lewis, Mrs., 90
Logia papyri, 109 f.
London Polyglot, 59
Lucian, edition of Septuagint, 141

Mace, W., edition of N.T., 61
Mai, Cardinal, 79
Manuscripts: the manuscript period, 6
— Chester Beatty papyri, 14, 28 f., 112 ff.
— Codex Alexandrinus, 14, 27, 31, 56 ff., 145, 148

Manuscripts: Codex Ambrosianus, 146
— — Bezæ, 46, 60, 65, 82, 132, 148
— — Claromontanus, 60, 65, 148
— — Ephraemi, 67, 146, 148
— — Laudianus, 65, 148
— — Marchalianus, 146
— — Sarravianus, 146
— — Sinaiticus, 14, 27, 31, 73-9, 82, 131, 145, 147
— — Vaticanus, 14, 27, 55, 64, 79, 82, 131, 145, 148
— Curetonian Syriac, 90
— Freer MSS., 98 ff.
— Koridethi Codex, 104, 132, 148
— Oxyrhynchus St. John, 28
— Sinaitic Syriac, 90 ff.
— Uncanonical Gospel, 1, 2
— Washington Codex of Deuteronomy and Joshua, 99, 146
— — — of Gospels, 100 ff., 107, 132, 148
    See also under several books of Bible
Matthaei, C. F., 62
Matthew's Bible (English), 49
Mazarin Bible (Latin), 42
Melito of Sardis, Chester Beatty papyrus of homily by, 117

Mill, J., textual apparatus to N.T., 60

Minuscule writing, 27, 40

Neutral (or Alexandrian) text of N.T., 82, 93, 128 ff., 142

New Testament books; how written and circulated, 35–7, 132 ff.; form of earliest MSS. of, 30

Numbers, Chester Beatty papyrus of, 114, 124, 146

Old Coptic (Sahidic) Version, 35, 111, 130, 147, 150

Old Latin Version, 35, 147, 149

Old Syriac Version, 35, 90, 130, 132, 139, 149

Old Testament, 6–19; dates of books, 8

Origen, 105, 140 f.

Oxyrhynchus Codex of St. John, 28

Palimpsest, 90

Papyrus as writing material, 20

Papyrus books, forms of, 21, 27 ff.; discoveries of, 21, 22

Papyrus fragments of N.T., 110

Paris Polyglot, 59

Pauline Epistles, Chester Beatty papyrus of, 29, 115 f., 120 ff., 148

Pentateuch, date of, 8

Peshitta Syriac Version, 41, 139, 147, 149

Polyglot Bibles, 59

Printed Hebrew Bible, 6; Greek Bible, 43 ff., 55

Printing, invention of, 42

"Received Text" of printed N.T., 45

Revelation, Chester Beatty papyrus of, 117, 122, 149

Revised Version, 81, 84 ff., 87

Rheims and Douai Bible (English), 51

Sahidic (Coptic) Version, 35, 111, 130, 147, 150

Samaritan Pentateuch, 15 ff.

Sanders, Prof. H. A., 115, 124

Sayings of Jesus, 109 f.

Schmidt, C., 112, 124

Scholz, J. M. A., list of MSS., 62

Semler, J. S., classification of MSS., 66

Septuagint, date and earliest MSS. of, 14; editions, 18

Simonides, C., 78

Sinaitic Syriac MS., 90 ff.

Soden, Prof. von, 104

Stephanus, Greek N.T. of 1550, 45, 60, 65; verse-division by, 50, 51 n.

Streeter, Canon B. H., 105

Syrian text of N.T., 83. *See also* s.v. Byzantine

Syro-Hexaplar Version of O.T., 147

Tatian. *See* s.v. Diatessaron

Tell el-Amarna tablets, 10

Theodotion, 18, 125

Tischendorf, C., 72–80

Tyndale, W., English printed Bibles of, 47 ff.

Uncanonical Gospel, fragment of, 1, 2

Uncial writing, 26, 40

Vellum, as writing material, 24 f.

Verses, division into, 50, 51

Versions of the Scriptures, importance of, 34

Vulgate, Latin, 41, 139 f., 147, 149

Walton, Bishop, Polyglot Bible of, 57, 59

Washington Codex of Deuteronomy and Joshua, 99, 146; of Gospels, 100 ff., 107, 122, 148

Wells, E., edition of N.T., 61

Westcott and Hort, 81 ff., 127, 129, 143

Western text of N.T., 82, 93, 128 ff., 138

Wetstein, J. J., list of MSS., 62

Writing, origins of, 9–11

Wyclif, English Bible of, 47

Ximenes, Cardinal, 43